A
TEAM
OF
LEADERS

A
TEAM
OF
LEADERS

Empowering Every Member to Take
Ownership, Demonstrate Initiative,
and Deliver Results

PAUL GUSTAVSON
AND
STEWART LIFF

AMACOM

AMERICAN MANAGEMENT ASSOCIATION

New York • Atlanta • Brussels • Chicago • Mexico City • San Francisco
Shanghai • Tokyo • Toronto • Washington, D.C.

Bulk discounts available. For details visit:
www.amacombooks.org/go/specialsales
Or contact special sales:
Phone: 800-250-5308
E-mail: specialsls@amanet.org
View all the AMACOM titles at: www.amacombooks.org
American Management Association: www.amanet.org

Library of Congress Cataloging-in-Publication Data

Gustavson, Paul.
   A team of leaders : empowering every member to take ownership, demonstrate initiative, and deliver results / Paul Gustavson and Stewart Liff.
      pages cm
   Includes bibliographical references and index.
   ISBN 978-0-8144-3407-9 — ISBN 0-8144-3407-X 1. Teams in the workplace. 2. Employee motivation. I. Liff, Stewart. II. Title.
   HD66.G876 2014
   658.4'022—dc23

                                                          2013042991

About AMA
American Management Association (www.amanet.org) is a world leader in talent development, advancing the skills of individuals to drive business success. Our mission is to support the goals of individuals and organizations through a complete range of products and services, including classroom and virtual seminars, webcasts, webinars, podcasts, conferences, corporate and government solutions, business books, and research. AMA's approach to improving performance combines experiential learning—learning through doing—with opportunities for ongoing professional growth at every step of one's career journey.

Printing number
10 9 8 7 6 5 4 3 2 1

Contents

Acknowledgments

WE COULD NOT HAVE written this book, of course, without the generosity of great mentors.

While playing football for Brigham Young University, I marveled at Hall of Fame coach LaVell Edwards and his methods for building a very good team. I count as one of the great blessings in my life to have been accepted into the BYU Masters of Organizational Behavior Program, where I had the privilege to be a teaching and research assistant to the late Bill Dyer, who in many circles is credited with being the "father of team building." Bill always encouraged me to write about what I was learning about teams. Now I am sure that Bill is smiling.

I am grateful to the late Forrest Belcher, who trusted and gave me his earliest opportunities to apply the team-building knowledge in the workplace while at Standard Oil of Indiana. Likewise, I am grateful for Federico Faggin and Manny Fernandez at Zilog, who encouraged and supported me in one of the first work innovations with teams in the high-tech industry, creating extraordinary results and a competitive advantage in manufacturing, product development, and customer service.

I am indebted to many clients over the years that provided me with great projects where building high-performance teams helped to create a strategic competitive advantage. These partnerships contributed to the development and refinement of many of the tools and techniques presented in this book.

I am also grateful for all those in his learning community who inspired and encouraged me to write about my experiences—Dave Ulrich, Kerry Patterson, Herb Stokes, John Cotter, Jim Taylor, Bronco Mendenhall, Norm Smallwood, Stephen M. R. Covey, Gibb Dyer, Ralph Christensen, Jeff Dyer, Craig Hunt, Michael Colemere, Richard Feller, Ann Henry, David Nielson, Claire Averett, Kreig Smith, Kyle Smith, Bret Thomas, Bill Scholz, May Speck, Mark Richards, Marc Swartz, Tom Ward, Tom Stone, Irv Rothman, Gerri Gold, Jim Tenner, Elliot Cooperstone, Starr Eckholdt, Bill Veltrop, Tim O'Hara, Shawn Brenchley, the late Cal Pava, Bonner Ritchie, Scott Jensen, Bruce Diamond, the late Steve Crossingham, and many others.

- Paul Gustavson

I would like to thank many of the people over the years that helped build my expertise in management and team development. They include Joe Thompson, Tom Lastowka, Rick Nappi, Nora Egan, Dave Walls, Ray Avent, John Vogel, Dan Kowalski, Paul Draper, Alan Checketts, Gary Turner, and Herman Greenspan.

I would like to acknowledge the contribution of Pamela A. Posey, D.B.A., to our joint work on visual management. For further details about visual management, see Stewart Liff and Pamela A. Posey, *Seeing Is Believing: How the New Art of Visual Management Can Boost Performance Throughout Your Organization* (New York: AMACOM, 2004), or visit www.stewartliff.com and www.EyesOnPerformance.com.

I would also like to thank Professors Harold Bruder, Gabriel Laderman, and Robert Bermelin, who greatly contributed to my education in the fine arts. Their teachings, combined with my business experience and continued growth, led to the concept of visual management as described in this book.

Finally, I would like to thank my many friends and colleagues over the years that helped open my eyes and provide me with the support and encouragement I needed to continue to grow. They include Dennis Kuewa, Pat Amberg-Blyskal, Barry Jackson, Ed Russell, Mike Harris, Bruce Petroff, Jenn Kler, Grant Singleton, Anne Haines, Lynda Russell, Ev Chasen, Veronica Wales, Monty Watson, Ventris Gibson, Susan Fishbein, Mike Walcoff, and Jeff Liff.

- Stewart Liff

Collectively, we would like to offer many thanks to our editors, Christina Parisi and Stephen Power, who guided us though the publication process, as well as to our other colleagues at AMACOM, all of whom provided wise advice and editorial support.

We would like to give special thanks to Elaine Biech for her untiring support and assistance on this project. We would also like to thank Scott Edelstein for his many insights and expertise on the entire publishing process.

We offer grateful thanks to our dear colleagues Mark Rhodes, Bill Snyder, and Alyson Von Feldt, who contributed deeply to our thinking and writing. We would also like to thank our colleagues at the Woodland's Group for the many years of intellectual stimulation and friendship they have provided us.

Finally, a big "hurrah" for Paul and Kris Anne's four children: Jule, Amber, April, and Jason, and to Stew and Lisa's family of six children: Rob, Jen, Marc, Matt, Rob C., and Amy. They were the ultimate test labs for these principles and concepts, and they are our most important teams. Each of them takes great interest in being a "team of leaders."

Our heartiest thanks go to Kris Anne and Lisa, our wives, who encouraged us to collaborate on a book for years and helped make this book-writing project a terrific experience.

A
TEAM
OF
LEADERS

THE OPPORTUNITY

How do you create an environment that successfully addresses the many challenges that supervisors and employees deal with while producing outstanding performance? The answer is simple: *You have to create an environment where everyone is a leader.* That is, an environment where everyone works together, takes the initiative, assumes ownership, is willing to deal with difficult issues, and accepts accountability for the team's results; an environment that is in stark contrast with one in which the supervisor tries to get everyone to produce.

This is a fundamental change in the way that most work entities operate. However, as we will show you, such a workplace design will produce better performance and make your work life much more exciting, enjoyable, and fulfilling.

You may think it sounds like a bunch of management buzzwords, concepts that are good in theory but virtually impossible to implement in the real world. However, plenty of organizations have already redesigned their workplaces using the principles, tools, techniques, and strategies that we explain to you in this book.

THE CHALLENGE

If you are a supervisor or a team leader, you know how difficult it is to run a unit or a team. You have constant pressure to perform, frequent demands on your time, problem employees to deal with, employees or unions with their own agendas … you get the picture.

You have the one job where everyone seems to give you a hard time—management demands improved performance, employees want you to solve their problems, the union thinks you are treating its constituents unfairly, other units need you to attend to their issues, and, by the way, your wife or husband and children would like some of your time as well. In short, you feel that the weight of the world often rests on your shoulders and you have few, if any, people to turn to for support. Deep down, you are probably saying to yourself, "There has got to be a better way."

As a team leader or team member, you most likely have stringent performance expectations and someone frequently looking over your shoulder. On top of that, you may feel these expectations are unrealistic and were simply imposed on you by higher-ups in management that don't understand or care what you are dealing with.

You might also be feeling out of the loop and disengaged because you don't know what is really going on or what your true purpose is.

Moreover, you may believe you are merely a cog in the wheel and easily replaceable, based on the whims of your superiors.

You may not like the way you are being treated and/or the way your team is being managed. For example, you may not be treated fairly, communication might be weak, and/or you may not receive the training you need. You may also feel you are not having the type of social connection with your coworkers that you would like to have.

Alternatively, you may feel that you are a star and part of a team of stars who, like a high-powered racing car, can do much more if given the opportunity. You yearn for a way to contribute in a higher and more rewarding manner.

For all the reasons stated and more, you and your coworkers may feel disenfranchised at work; the result is low morale, turned-off employees, and, most important, poor performance. That is exactly why companies have invested millions, if not billions, of dollars in training, organizational and team development.

The challenges/problems just described, and which you are probably experiencing, are most likely caused by the traditional work structure. That structure involves units or teams of people supervised by one individual who is over his head. To make matters worse, this structure is typically supported by a series of management systems and processes that are designed to maintain that relationship and unintentionally keep *you* and others from becoming a leader.

In other words, most units/teams are designed *not to produce leaders,* which results in people thinking and acting simply as workers. Does this assessment apply to your situation? We suspect that it probably does.

Before we go forward, we want to be clear that we are not saying it is impossible to have a successful team or unit using a traditional structure. Obviously you can. What we are saying is that with 1) all the inherent challenges that currently exist in the workplace, and 2) the expectation that things will only get more complicated, if you have a team of committed leaders, you are much more likely to have a high-performing team that will not be bogged down with all the negative issues we previously described.

Many organizations have tried to address these issues, at least to some extent, by converting to a team environment. Perhaps yours has. The degree to which this team-building effort has helped matters varies, of course, case by case. However, relatively few organizations have tried to build *teams of leaders,* believing it is unrealistic or too difficult to accomplish, or they simply didn't know how to get there. As a result, the traditional supervisor–employee relationship remains largely intact, and the aforementioned challenges have only been addressed to a limited degree, at best.

IS THERE A MODEL WE CAN USE TO BUILD A TEAM OF LEADERS?

The one we recommend is the Five-Stage Team Development Model, which is the underlying foundation of this book (our discussion of this model was influenced by the work of Carl A. Bramlette Jr. and Abe Raab). This model identifies the five distinct stages of team development. At Stage One (the way most units/teams work today), the team leader interacts with each team member, one-on-one. The model goes on to describe how your team can evolve and grow in varying stages all the way up to Stage Five. This is the stage where the team essentially manages itself, everyone becomes a leader, and the supervisor's time is freed up to work in other areas that create more value.

Imagine being the leader of a team that is at Stage Five. Under this scenario, you would advise the team as needed but spend most of your time working on higher, cross-functional, and outside issues. Many of the problems that you typically deal with would now be handled by the team itself, freeing you up to work at a broader level.

Your relationship with the team would also be very different. Instead of being a traditional supervisor who manages people on a one-on-one basis, you would teach the team members how to handle these issues and be available to assist them as needed. Instead of being frequently bogged down and overwhelmed, you would now have the time to focus on the important issues that were often neglected.

Perhaps most important, instead of pushing and cajoling a disparate group of individuals to work on the team's goals and objectives, you will be working with energetic and motivated individuals who are leaders in their own right, and who will only occasionally turn to you for help in order to take them to the next level. They will not be a group of whiners or people looking after their own best interests. Instead, they will be a team of leaders, trying to push the envelope and striving for the best performance possible. Wouldn't that be a refreshing change?

If you are a team member, imagine what it would be like to be part of a team of leaders at Stage Five. You would be a valued member of a team that manages itself. Instead of having someone standing over you cracking the whip, you would now be part of a cohesive team wherein everyone holds each other accountable.

In lieu of having goals simply imposed on you, you would play an integral role in developing these goals and trying to achieve them. Instead of hoping that you get the training you need to do your job, you would be involved in developing a comprehensive training plan to both gather and disseminate critical job knowledge.

Rather than wondering where you fit in the organization, what you contribute, and what your team's purpose is, you would know exactly where you fit, understand the value you contribute, and have a clear sense of purpose.

You would also work within a framework that is clear and aligned, meaning you would receive messages that are both consistent and purposeful. Furthermore, you would work in a setting that provides a strong social network and offers you the camaraderie and support you crave. Finally, you would work in a physical environment that is both inspiring and informational and reinforces your connection to both the mission and the metrics. Wouldn't that be an amazing change from your current situation?

EXAMPLES OF TEAMS THAT HAVE SUCCEEDED AT SELF-MANAGEMENT

You're probably still wondering, "Is it possible after all? Can it work in the real world?"

Let's review two examples of organizations that converted to self-directed work teams using the Five-Stage Model. As you are reviewing these examples, compare them with the way your unit/team operates.

The General Electric plant in Durham, North Carolina, does final assembly for the GE90 and CF34 jet engines. A *Fast Company* article, "Engines of Democracy," pointed out that the plant's real power lies in the way that work is performed.[1]

The plant has more than 300 employees[2] but only one boss—the plant manager. All of these employees report to the boss, meaning that for all intents and purposes, they have no supervisor. Self-directed teams build the jet engines—teams that decide how to manage the work, how to manage time off, how to improve systems and work processes, and how to deal with problem teammates.

Pay is transparent—that is, everyone is aware of how much money others on the team make because employees are paid by their skill level, and that information is available to each employee.

The teams do not maintain a typical assembly line. Instead, they own an engine from start to finish. Moreover, everyone's work varies on a daily basis, keeping the work interesting and resulting in a high degree of variety.

This plant has no time clock, so team members can take care of their personal business when needed. Meanwhile, the plant manager—the only supervisor in the entire plant—sits in an open cubicle in the middle of the factory floor.

As you might expect, everyone does not successfully fit into this environment, especially "people who expect to take orders." That is because the plant was designed to be operated by teams of leaders. To put that into perspective, there's this comment from one of the team members at the time the *Fast Company* article was written: "I have fifteen bosses … All of my teammates are my bosses."[3]

The people in the Durham plant are clearly engaged, have high energy, possess multiple skills, and are very motivated. In addition, they take tremendous pride in their team and the work they perform. More important, the plant's performance has continued to excel and it is considered by many to be an industry leader. All of this did not occur simply by magic.

Oh, and by the way, when the GE plant first started out on its transformation effort, the plant had 175 employees. Since then, the workforce has virtually doubled and GE continues to invest in the plant. Does that sound like your current situation?

Our second example pertains to government, a sector in which change is always difficult. Both of the authors worked together on this endeavor to transform one particular organization and its teams.

Department of Veterans Affairs regional offices are responsible for adjudicating claims for veterans benefits. All told, the VA has fifty-eight regional offices across the country serving more than 24 million veterans.

In 1986, Stew became the assistant director of the U.S. Department of Veterans Affairs New York Regional Office (NYRO). At the time, all regional offices processed claims for benefits using an assembly-line approach, resulting in many errors, a large amount of rework, and no one really owning the claim. Moreover, teamwork was rarely emphasized since there were many specialized jobs and employees were only measured on how well they handled their small piece of the process.

From the perspective of veterans, the claims took much too long to process. (They still do, as VA has been overwhelmed with hundreds of thousands of claims from veterans returning from Iraq and Afghanistan.) But veterans voiced other complaints as well. For example, they found it extremely difficult to find out the status of their claims, and they did not have a central point of contact. Naturally, this situation led to a high degree of frustration and low customer satisfaction.

In 1991, a new director, Joe Thompson, arrived. He felt that the system was archaic and there had to be a better way to process claims, serve veterans, and manage the employees. Working closely with OPD (Paul's company), Thompson, along with Stew and the NYRO's staff, transformed the office from a unit-based operation to a team-based environment. Supervisors were replaced with or became coaches, and the team members received an enormous amount of technical training, as well as training on how to operate as a self-managed team.

The assembly-line process was replaced with each team owning the claims under its jurisdiction, resulting in fewer handoffs, more knowledgeable and better-developed employees, and veterans having one point of contact.

Service was measured using a balanced scorecard, which meant productivity, timeliness, and quality weren't looked at in a vacuum any longer. Along these lines, this information was posted and shared with the employees.

All processes were reviewed (e.g., the way people were interviewed, the manner in which performance was reviewed and managed, the way people were paid), and changes were made where appropriate.

The NYRO even built a museum of veterans benefits on-site, in order for employees to connect more closely to the mission. Eventually, people began to think and act differently as they evolved from being merely workers to becoming leaders.

As word spread of this transformation effort, many public and private sector organizations came to learn from the NYRO's experience.

Eventually, its success resulted in the NYRO receiving the first Hammer Award for reinventing government from then Vice President Al Gore.[4]

Stew and many of his teammates remember this as perhaps the most magical time of their careers. People came to work excited, feeling they had been elevated, had a higher sense of purpose, and were doing something special. They worked together in a way that is rarely seen in a work setting, particularly government.

Today, roughly twenty years after that transformation effort, many of the members of the senior team keep in touch and consider each other to be lifelong friends. Wouldn't you like to feel that way about your team?

NOW WHAT?

Since most problems are caused by the way teams and their management systems and processes are *designed*, in order to address the problems once and for all, teams need to change their design. For example, if your team is designed to operate under a supervisor who is all-knowing and all-controlling, you will react accordingly. That is, you will probably overrely on your supervisor, be afraid to exercise independent judgment, not show much initiative, and be merely a follower.

If little information is shared, you will not know what value you contribute or understand the effect of your actions, in which case the unintended consequences are going to be low productivity and/or downstream errors. Meanwhile, the supervisor will have to frequently work to the point of exhaustion, since she will be trying to control the work of a group of compliant (but not committed) employees, which is a formula for mediocrity at best.

The point here is that you get what you design for; if you want to have a team of leaders, you must design and align all your systems and processes to make that happen.

Since it probably took your team/unit a number of years to get to where it is today, expect that it will take some time, perhaps even years, before your team can become a Stage Five team. A good analogy here is weight control: Just as it takes time to gain weight, it also takes time to lose it. Moreover, unless the requisite support systems are in place (e.g., exercise, eating right, a calorie counter if necessary), you are unlikely to keep the weight off in the long run.

The same concept holds true for taking your team to Stage Five: It takes time to get there, and your transformation will only last if the necessary systems and processes are in place. However, the results will definitely make your investment of time and energy worthwhile!

So, a core principle of this book is that you should design your team for the results you want. The rest of this book will show you how to do just that.

Creating Advantage Through the Five-Stage Team Development Model

***Key principle:** Leadership always exists in a team; however, everyone becomes a leader once a team achieves Stage Five of the Five-Stage Team Development Model.*

THINK OF YOUR CURRENT team or work unit. Is it self-managing? How involved and committed are your team members? How well do you all work together? How many people act as leaders? How much knowledge is shared? Most important, how well is your team/unit performing? If you are using a traditional supervisor–employee model, we strongly suspect that your answers to most, if not all, of these questions will be lukewarm at best.

Our experience and research has shown that the highest performing teams exhibit more self-sufficiency (i.e., self-management) and are more engaged than leader-focused teams. This makes perfect sense because self-managing teams have a greater sense of ownership and employee involvement and often produce better results. While many of the same principles, strategies, tactics, tools, and frameworks generally apply to all types of teams, only well-developed, self-managing teams produce teams of leaders.

If your team is not self-managing and is not producing the results you would like, then this is the time to explore a proven, alternative approach.

SELF-MANAGED WORK TEAMS

A self-managed team is a team of employees working on their own toward a common goal, whose members identify, plan, and manage their daily activities and work under very limited or no supervision. As the team develops, the members do, too, with one of the key objectives being to transform each employee into a committed, highly engaged, flexible, and well-rounded leader.

High-performing self-managed teams retain much greater accountability for their work. Because they often are cross-trained, they are better at problem solving and more flexible in meeting scheduling requirements. In general, multifunctional teams control variances in the process better than functional "silos" because they are more aware of the downstream effects of their mistakes.

To become self-managing, each of your team's members must learn how to accomplish many new tasks, such as planning, scheduling, and performance feedback—tasks that are traditionally performed by supervisors. It's not an easy thing to do. In fact, a common mistake organizations make is to expect work teams to become high-performing right away.

Rather, self-managed teams evolve over a period of months or, more often, years. So don't be surprised if a temporary drop in productivity or morale first precedes the benefits you reap from becoming such a team, as people struggle to change. This book is important because it will explain why the transition is often difficult; at the same time, we will show you how to make the journey as effective and painless as possible.

Once your team truly becomes self-managing, you can expect to deliver improved performance. Moreover, individual results within your team will also get better because people will find the challenge of learning new kinds of management tasks to be very rewarding. Finally, as each team member's role evolves and as your team members become more engaged, possess wider and deeper skills, and start being proactive, they will change from being merely doers to becoming energetic leaders.

THE TEAM DEVELOPMENT MODEL

To accomplish the ambitious goals described, we will focus on one of the real breakthrough tools used by teams to separate themselves from the pack. This framework and tool (influenced by the work of Carl A. Bramlette Jr. and Abe Raab) was discovered when trying to facilitate the natural propensity and desire of team members to move toward building increased capability and self-management.

The Five-Stage Team Development Model allows self-managed teams to develop over time vis-à-vis their relationship with their leader. As teams become more independent, team leaders in turn are freed up to do more development and analysis work. Understanding this development process will make your transition to self-managing teams much smoother.

FIGURE 1-1. The starting point of team development.

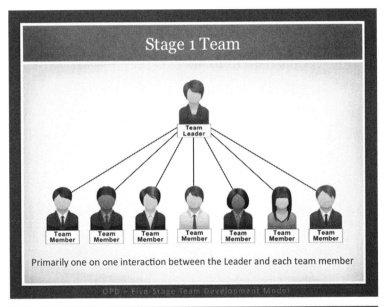

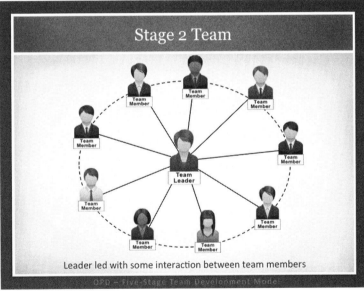

FIGURE 1-1. The starting point of team development. *(continued)*

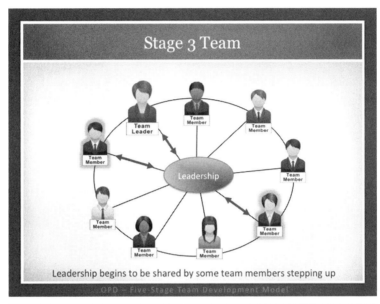

continue

FIGURE 1-1. The starting point of team development. *(continued)*

A successful self-managed team generally evolves through a series of discernible stages. As you can see in Figure 1-1, at the first stage, your team will start off with virtually every key decision being made by the supervisor or team leader. Because the transition to self-management is going to require a lot of change, the team needs an enormous amount of support.

Some of the initial enthusiasm often gives way to sarcasm as things will not go as smoothly as many people expect. This is why the team leader must be more involved than ever—to ensure that people understand how teams evolve, to address areas of uncertainty, and to deal with issues that the team is not capable of handling.

Slowly, your team will become less leader-focused. As the team moves to Stage Two, it will start to grapple with what its goals and objectives are and try to ensure that everyone is on the same page. Again, this transition usually doesn't happen as quickly as many would like. The team leader will still have to do a lot of coordinating and mentoring as the team begins to take baby steps while the leader begins to gradually move away from exercising full authority.

Stage Three is the midway point in your team's evolution. While there still may be some frustration, members will start to learn their roles and come together. The "big picture" starts to become clearer to the team and its members, and a few individuals will even step up and provide some limited but real leadership. Moreover, the team will start to focus on performance. At the same time, this is also the stage where your team will start to deal with difficult people issues. The supervisor still will be intimately involved in helping to resolve these challenges, because team members usually don't know what to do and are uncomfortable with conflict. (Interestingly, dealing with difficult people is something that most supervisors are not usually comfortable with, either.)

At Stage Four, your team will really start to hum. Most of the team members are able to step up and lead in at least one specific area. People will communicate quite well and learn from each other. They will also take a serious interest in performance and try and actively achieve many of their goals and objectives. In addition, the level of engagement will clearly rise and the team will look to take charge of all its key processes and procedures. By the same token, there will still be work to do, particularly in the areas of problem solving and conflict resolution—two areas that teams generally take longer to become proficient in. You must also continue to work on ensuring that all the team members have the requisite skill sets. At this stage, the supervisor will now be more of a coach and be on a more equal footing with the other team members, and the primary focus becomes training and developing the team members. He will have time to begin to focus on higher order work and contributions.

Once your team reaches Stage Five, it will be at the highest level where the team is self-managing. You will now work together as a unit to set and achieve a challenging set of goals and objectives. Everyone will be involved in team management and in grabbing the bull by the horns in order to get the job done. More important, individual team members will no longer be followers—they will be leaders who look down the road and at their environment in order to get and stay ahead of the curve. Meanwhile, good performance will no longer be acceptable to your team members—they will only accept excellent performance and beyond. Finally, the energy level of the team will be extremely high as its members will know what they need to do, will be committed to doing it, and will work together to provide the best performance possible.

All of this change will allow you, as team leader, to focus on other things besides team performance. Now the leader becomes more of a peripheral member of the team and is free to work on larger issues such as analysis, planning, and cross-functional concerns. Figure 1-2 describes the five stages of this team development model. It depicts 1) the changing roles of the team members and the leader and 2) how everyone becomes a leader.

As you can clearly see, at Stage Five, where everyone is a leader, the roles are strikingly different. People are no longer workers; they are all actively involved in every aspect of the team's operation. Wouldn't you want to be part of a team where everyone is this involved and committed, and where the supervisor actually has time to both scan the environment and look down the road?

FIGURE 1-2. Five-Stage Team Development Model: How everyone becomes a leader.

Stage	Team Members' Role	Team Leader's Role
One: Being directive	Receives assignments and follows orders.	Traditional; makes assignments one-on-one with each member of the team.
Two: Journey starts	Employees begin to interact with each other and start to learn new team processes.	Supervisor begins to coach the team (i.e., begins to develop the team and the team members).
Three: Progress	Leadership begins to be shared. A few team members step up and provide leadership on tasks and assignments. Codifiable knowledge sharing is increasing. The team is starting to see the bigger picture.	Supervisor identifies areas where team members can step up and take on leadership responsibilities and coaches those who desire to successfully step up on these leadership activities. Continues to lead on most of the leadership activities while accelerating learning and the transfer of responsibilities.
Four: Almost there	Leadership is shared. Most team members are stepping up and taking responsibility for the majority of the leadership activities. Many beginning to focus on increasing the value of their own and their team's contribution. Some tacit knowledge is being shared.	Team leader has delegated the majority of leadership activities that the team members can handle and plays the role of counselor and coach to those who have stepped up. The team leader also becomes involved with high-value work outside the team and begins transitioning difficult people issues to the team.
Five: Everyone a leader	Everyone on the team steps up and provides leadership so that all the leadership tasks are led by the team members. Many team members can lead multiple activities and are leaders on all issues. They are pushing their performance to the next level. Codifiable and tacit knowledge equally shared. Long-term planning is being done. Outstanding performance is the result.	The leader becomes adviser to the team as team members take their performance to the next level. Remains the person to whom the team reports on its accountabilities. The team leader's greatest contribution comes from being involved with higher-level work (looking outward, special projects, cross-functional teams, etc.) and managing multiple teams.

To make things even clearer, Figure 1-3 is a detailed guide to help you better understand the way your team will develop.

Now that we have explained the model from several different perspectives, let's take a step back and look at several examples of the way teams might evolve under the model.

EXAMPLE: SPECIAL TEAMS UNIT

Our first real-world example is a college football team's Special Teams Unit. Special Teams Units handle kicking plays such as punts, field goals, and kickoffs. Here is how a team expected its unit to develop at each stage.

Stage One

- Special team members understand their objectives through direct instruction from their coach on the field and in meetings.

- Special team members give ideas and recommendations to their coach.

- The coach reviews and interprets special team results and determines priorities and necessary actions, as well as communicates this information either at team meetings or practices (which the coach leads) or in one-on-one meetings.

- The coach determines the depth chart and who is or isn't getting the job done.

- The coach retains most of the ownership of the success or failure of the special team's performance, schemes, and techniques.

FIGURE 1-3. Guide to the Five-Stage Team Development Model.

Stage I	Stage II	Stage III	Stage IV	Stage V
Primarily one on one interaction between the manager and each team member.	*Manager leads team with interaction between team members*	*Leadership begins to be shared where some team members are stepping up and providing leadership to key team processes and activities while engaging other team member participation.* *The manager plays an important coaching role to assist individual team members to step up into leadership roles.*	*Leadership is shared where most of the team members are stepping up and providing leadership on key team processes and activities while engaging other team member participation.* *The manager plays an important coaching role to take the team to the next level but has time to step up to do higher-level work.*	*Leadership is shared, all team members are stepping up another level in leadership of processes and activities, setting and attaining challenging performance targets, benchmarking and establishing best practices, and leading and contributing to other teams.* *The manager's time is freed up to step up to do higher-level work outside the team but is still available to the team for counsel.*
• The formal leader interacts with members of the team primarily through one-on-one interaction. Interaction is one-way street.	• The formal leader leads and directs the team primarily through team meetings and activities.	• A few members of the team are "stepping up" and providing leadership in areas that the formal leader was previously leading.	• Most everyone is stepping up in at least one or more of the key leadership activities.	• Everyone is stepping up.
• Interaction might resemble a "pipe" where the communication and direction setting on performance targets, work assignments, and accountabilities are provided in one-on-one top-down settings.	• The team transitions to more like a "hub" with the formal leader in the center directing and responding to input from its members.	• The formal leader continues to provide most of the direction to the team but encourages and supports members in "stepping up".	• The team is performing at a high level.	• Everyone is capable of stepping up on most if not all of the leadership activities.
• The individual's role is to understand what, when, and how the work assignments are to be done primarily in one-and-one interactions with the formal leader. In these one-on-one interactions the individual team member is expected to contribute input and insights as well as ask questions for clarification. Interaction is not a one-way street.	• The members tend to rely on the formal leader for clarity of work assignments and setting objectives needed to accomplish.	• The team continues to perform more as individual members on a team, but there begins to be some team ownership of certain areas of responsibility.	• The team works together to set performance targets and track and improve them. The team begins to own more of its performance and operate as a self-sufficient team but still needs the formal leader's help on a few items.	• The team is performing at a very high level.
• The formal leader feels strong accountability for setting targets and achieving results both by the team and by each individual. Individuals feel responsible for their own work and results.	• The formal leader takes responsibility for the development of the members of the team and does this both in a team environment as well as in one-on one-settings.	• Performance targets continue to be set by the formal leader; however, the team begins to take leadership in tracking and suggesting improvements to performance.	• The team collaborates and shares knowledge at a higher level.	• The team sets stretch performance targets and achieves them.
	• In team settings, the members begin to interact with each other and coordinate planning work assignments and sharing insights and knowledge with each other.	• The formal leader feels very accountable for the team's performance, but a few others are beginning to feel it also.	• The team leader transitions to a role more as a coach to the team rather than directing the team's day-to-day activities.	• The team is accountable and owns its performance as a team.
	• The formal leader feels accountable for the team's performance and the individuals feel accountable for their performance.	• Members of the team work on increasing their capabilities as individuals as well as learning skills in order to "step up".	• The formal leader's time begins to be freed up to do higher-value work or begin to manage multiple teams.	• The team benchmarks best practices and learns and applies where appropriate in their process or community of practice.
			• The formal leader coaches the team towards' Stage Five and helps individuals build more leadership capabilities.	• The team helps coach other teams desirous to be a Stage Five team. They document and share their best practices openly.
				• The formal leader's time is freed up to do higher-value work or manage multiple teams.
				• The formal leader is still available as a resource to the team as it stretches its targets and capabilities.

Stage Two

- Special team members understand their objectives and regularly watch films to review their results.

- The coach leads special team performance review meetings and helps team members to better understand and interpret why they achieved their performance results.

- Team members provide input and discuss results.

- Team members begin to take some responsibility for following up with each other and communicating what can be done to improve and what was talked about in the special teams meetings with the coach.

- Players take some initiative to learn what will help the special teams excel, but the coach continues to determine the depth chart, identify problem performance, and teach schemes and techniques.

Stage Three

- The coaching staff selects special team captains and they begin to take responsibility for certain activities, such as assimilation, training, and performance management.

- Under the direction of the coach, the special team captains recommend special team members (with input from team members) and determine the depth chart, but final approval rests with the coach.

- Special team members undertake the important work of reviewing and analyzing reports and film regularly, while the special team captains run specific team performance review meetings to interpret the results, with help from the coach.

- Special team members are able to identify players they trust to get the job done and provide input to their special team captain. The coach still provides help to sort out the right priorities of each team.

- The coach coordinates with the other areas of the team to make sure the special teams are optimizing their performance; the coach helps facilitate difficult meetings and practices to ensure that time is used effectively.

Stage Four

- The special team captains own the priorities and performance leadership of their teams and follow up as appropriate.

- Facilitated by the special team captains, the special team unit reviews its performance results on a regular basis, with oversight by the coach; only now the players motivate one another.

- The special team owns not only the selection of its members and depth chart, but also the assimilation, training, and performance management of its team members, with some counsel from the coach.

- Others on the team begin to build leadership capability that will allow them to take on the role of the special team captains.

- The coach helps in refreshing certain techniques, schemes, and plays as well as introducing new techniques, schemes, plays, and skills.

Stage Five

- The special team consistently exceeds its performance objectives.

- Special team captains facilitate the process of staffing the special teams with input from their team members and, when needed, counsel from the coach.

- The role of special team captain rotates among the members of the team, with more and more individuals capable of providing leadership. The team selects its own captains.

- The special team fully owns not only the selection of its members and depth chart, but also the assimilation, training, and performance management of team members.

- Special team members consult with other teams to learn best practices/techniques for improving team performance. Analyzing trends in performance enables them to do daily and weekly planning, as well as longer-term planning.

- Team members are able to plan and manage cross-team activities to ensure alignment and proper integration.

- Team members continue to rely on their coach to scan the outside environment for leading-edge techniques, schemes, and practices that can be brought back to the team in order to further enhance their performance; whenever possible, they are involved in some of these activities.

While the mission of the football Special Teams Unit is probably very different from your team's, interestingly, this team followed the same basic evolutionary stages as teams in other fields, including manufacturing and service industries. In the example, team members decided that they could improve by changing the roles and responsibilities within the team. The net result was that the players became much more involved in the planning of the unit's activities, developed a greater stake in its outcome, and ultimately produced better results than under the traditional model. The key was that they received nurturing and support in their development, and they were given time to facilitate their transition.

EXAMPLE: SENIOR LEADERSHIP TEAM

To reinforce but not belabor the point, let's look at a less detailed evolution of a senior leadership team that is comprised of the heads of a series of management councils.

Stage One. The team works primarily through one-on-one interaction between the leader and each management council member. During this stage, the council heads take their marching orders from the presiding leader.

Stage Two. The team is still leader-led, but there is growing interaction between council members. Council members begin to do more than simply follow orders.

Stage Three. Leadership begins to be shared; some council members are stepping up and providing leadership to key council processes and activities while engaging other council members.

Stage Four. Leadership is now shared, with most of the council members providing leadership on key team processes and activities while being actively involved with other council members and getting their participation. The presiding leader plays an important coaching role to take the team to the next level but has time to do higher-level work.

Stage Five. Leadership is fully shared; all council members are stepping up another level in leadership of processes and activities. They are setting and attaining challenging performance targets, benchmarking, establishing best practices, and leading and contributing to other councils. The presiding leader's time is freed up to do higher-level work outside the team, but this individual is still available to the team for counsel.

As you can see, the principles and evolution of a self-managed team are the same, regardless of whether you are dealing with a senior team of managers, a football team, a white-collar team, a manufacturing team, or even a family. If you want to have a self-managing team, you must progress through a defined series of stages toward self-management. But, in order to do this, you must have the requisite design, processes, tools, and support systems in place—otherwise, frustration and chaos are likely to ensue. The remaining chapters of this book will show you how to set up these designs, processes, and systems.

UNDERSTANDING WHERE YOUR TEAM IS

Now that we have described and illustrated the Five-Stage Team Development Model, let's see what you have learned and how you can apply this information.

We'll start by presenting additional examples of teams at different stages of development (not necessarily in order). Read them and tease them out. Act like a social anthropologist and examine the clues contained in the next five examples and then decide which stage the team is in. This exercise will help you improve your understanding of team development and help you apply the methodology, offered later in this chapter, to your own team.

As you read each example, keep in mind that a good analogy is the development of a human being. People also move through predictable phases—baby, toddler, child, teenager, and finally, adult.

Here's our first example.

John is a member of a distribution services team. He is standing at his workstation staring at his machine. The frustration level is welling up inside of him. He just observed Eric walk in the door. For the third time this week, Eric is forty-five minutes late for work. As a result, the team probably won't reach its production numbers for any of these days. John mentioned the situation to his teammates two days ago at break time. Everyone else was as frustrated as John was. They talked pretty tough about what should be done with Eric. But, when the conversation was over, even John agreed that it was the supervisor's job to deal with Eric.

I thought we were supposed to "step up," John kept thinking to himself. That's what he heard everyone talking about in the all-employee meeting. In his heart he knew the team's supervisor would do what he has always done with Eric—pretty much ignore the situation. *At best he'll slap him on the back and ask him if he knows what time work starts,* thought John.

At what stage do you think John's team is at? Why? What key phrases helped you determine the stage you picked?

Answer: The team is at Stage One. The team is still leader-centric. By and large, team members have not yet stepped up; they expect their supervisor/leader to handle teamwide issues. Two key phrases helped us reach that conclusion:

John agreed that it was the supervisor's job to deal with Eric.

"I thought we were supposed to 'step up.'"

These phrases indicate that the team members are still looking to the supervisor to solve the team's problems. They also demonstrate that there is a lot of confusion regarding everyone's roles and responsibilities. In a sense, the team is at the "baby" phase of its evolution.

So how does this example apply to your team? What stage are you at? What strategies would you apply to take the team to the next stage?

Here's our next example.

Dan is a member of one of the teams in the finance and budget department. Tomorrow, Dan will be stepping up and conducting the weekly team meeting for the first time. Before e-mailing the agenda to the rest of the team, Dan does a quick check to make sure he has all the information necessary to support tomorrow's agenda:

- Reporting schedule for next week
- Budget work the team has to finish
- Name of the community service project the department will support

Dan tells a fellow team member, Pino, that he really appreciates the effort of all the team members to get their input to him on time. This helps to get the agenda out promptly so that the team has an opportunity to prepare for the meeting.

The finance and budget team has also been picked to make a presentation on its budget and forecasting techniques. This is something Dan's team has gotten pretty good at, along with a couple of other areas.

One thing Dan is not very excited about is conducting a corrective action meeting, although he recognizes eventually the team needs to step up and tackle this issue. The team is holding such a meeting on Friday with Ed, a fairly new team member who transferred in earlier in the year. He has been late in completing his assignments and isn't completely aligned with the program, in spite of the team's efforts to encourage and talk to him about his behavior. *Not all aspects of stepping up are fun*, Dan thinks to himself. *We have a lot to learn from our supervisor Randy, who will be leading the meeting on how to deal with Ed's behavior before the problem gets worse*, he concludes. *We are stepping up in a couple of areas, but our supervisor believes we need to develop our leadership skills so that we can all 'step up' in many more ways.*

At what stage do you think Dan's team is at? Why? What key phrases helped you determine the stage you picked?

Answer: The team is at Stage Three. The team is beginning to come together, at least to a certain extent. Individual team members are starting to deal with some of the tough stuff and are also recognizing they need to learn from their supervisor and develop additional leadership skills.

In essence, they have become like children. They are no longer as needy as before and are starting to exert some independence, but they still need a lot of support and guidance.

Here are the key phrases from the story that helped us reach that conclusion:

Tomorrow, Dan will be stepping up and conducting the weekly team meeting.

"Not all aspects of stepping up are fun," Dan thinks to himself. "We have a lot to learn from our supervisor Randy."

"We are stepping up in a couple of areas."

"We need to develop our leadership skills so that we can all 'step up' in many more ways."

How does this example apply to your team? Is your team at or near this stage? Why? What strategies would you apply to take the team to the next stage? What help might be needed?

Here is our third example.

Phyllis, a fairly new supervisor for one of the teams in the Global Service Center, is sitting at her kitchen table. She had no idea that being a supervisor could be so trying and frustrating. Her team has a lot of potential and has great people on it, but there are lots of challenges ahead. The team just finished working on goals and objectives. *What a struggle that was. Trying to get the team members to participate was like pulling teeth*, Phyllis mused to herself.

"I can hardly wait until everyone at least understands the work processes," Phyllis says to her husband, Mark. "That will really take some of the pressure off. After that, maybe we can spend more time on social skills—they sure need it," she continued. Mark reminds Phyllis that just last week she said that the team was making some progress and production was improving. "That's a good point," Phyllis concedes. "However, it consumes a lot of my time to coordinate everything and do all the tutoring that needs to be done, but it is rewarding to see the team begin to get a sense of what being a 'team' is all about, like asking each other for help and encouraging each other," Phyllis tells Mark. "Just be patient," Mark says. "You are learning a great deal, and so is your team."

Where do you think this team is in its evolution? Why? What key phrases helped you determine the stage you picked?

Answer: The team is at Stage Two. A few members of the team are just starting to take on additional responsibility, and they are also beginning to work together—at least to a limited extent—but the supervisor is still stretched too thin.

The team is still very young and struggling, but it is beginning to take some steps forward—in other words, the human equivalent of a toddler. Several key phrases helped us reach that conclusion:

The team just finished working on goals and objectives.

"It consumes a lot of my time to coordinate everything and do all the tutoring that needs to be done," Phyllis says.

The team is beginning "to get a sense of what being a 'team' is all about, like asking each other for help and encouraging each other."

So, how does this example relate to your team? Is your team at or near this stage and dealing with similar issues? Why? What strategies would you apply to take the team to the next stage? What help might you need?

Here is our fourth example.

Ralph and Barbara, members of the distribution services leadership team, are conversing with each other before their team meeting starts. Barbara is telling Ralph how much she enjoyed his presentation on the organization's new supply chain strategy. The team believes the information will be very helpful in preparing for its goal-setting session coming up in a week. Barbara is amused that the distribution services manager is concerned that their team may be setting targets and standards too high. But, according to Barbara, he has to remember that they met the targets they set in their last two annual planning cycles.

The new technology the team recommended last week, and won support for, will enhance performance and improve service levels. They would have fallen behind industry standards without it. The team and its members were pretty proud of themselves. They really had their "ducks lined up" for the presentation they made to the budget committee. They scanned the environment for best practices and to understand industry benchmarks before they made their technology recommendation and established their targets. Area managers were impressed with the team's environmental scan data. The interviews they videotaped with their customers have been circulated throughout their organization and the areas. It opened a few eyes, to say the least.

Following today's team meeting, Barbara's team will be conducting training on performance management and stepping up with one of the newer teams in another area that started up six months ago. She remembers that Duncan, her manager, just returned from a meeting of the Global Materials Committee. He's able to serve on the committee nearly full-time because he now has more time to step up and do more global work in the same way that all the team members are "stepping up" in their team roles. Barbara thought to herself, *I'll share our training outline with Duncan. He may have seen or heard about a global best practice that I could leverage or link into. Maybe we can discuss that after the team meeting.*

Where do you think this team is in its evolution? Why? What key phrases helped you determine the stage you picked?

Answer: The team is at Stage Five. The team is truly self-managing, high performing, and striving to get even better. Individuals are all stepping up and operating as a real team, which has allowed their manager to begin working on cross-organizational issues. Moreover, everyone is now functioning as a leader.

The team is now the equivalent of a mature adult—standing on its own two feet and meeting the world head-on.

Here are the key phrases that helped us reach that conclusion:

The team may be setting targets and standards too high. But the distribution services manager has to remember that they met the targets they set in their last two annual planning cycles.

They scanned their environment for best practices and to understand industry benchmarks.

Duncan, the manager, had more time to step up and do more global work in the same way that all the team members are "stepping up" in their team roles.

How do you view this example in relation to your team? Is your team anywhere near this magical stage? Why? What strategies would you apply to ensure that your team keeps going in the right direction? What help might you need?

This next story is our final example.

George, a member of the leadership team for physical facilities, drops a bunch of papers as he races down the hall. As he stoops over to pick them all up, he notices David, the VP of operations, coming over to help him.

"Where are you going in such a hurry?" David asks.

"I'm on my way to an interview planning meeting. Our department has approval to contract out some of our work that truly doesn't differentiate us and I'm on the selection committee to interview outside vendors," George replies.

"I thought you just hired some new people in your department," David says, pretty emphatically.

"That's true; that was four months ago," George states. "It was for work that we determined is the kind of unique work we should be more involved with, and we weren't sized appropriately."

"Is your team going to participate in the on-boarding/assimilation process of the new vendor also?" David asks.

"As a matter of fact," George says, "we are already planning that now because we know how important good handoffs are in a transition. Jen, our human resources manager, has been partnering with us to do more and more of the on-boarding/assimilation of employees and we thought we would use some best practices she taught us. We're not quite ready to do it all on our own, so we still need help from Jen and others. But we are close. We have enjoyed the opportunity to step up, and now the majority of the team is able to lead at least one of our critical work activities, albeit still with some good periodic coaching from our manager, Heinz.

"Well, I better get going, David. Good to see you again," George hurriedly adds as he turns to run to the interviews.

Where do you think this team is now in its evolution? Why? What phrases did you cull from the story that helped you determine the stage you picked?

Answer: The team is at Stage Four. While the team is approaching self-management, it's not there yet. Most, but not all, team members can assume a leadership role. While the team manager is able to distance himself from the team to some extent, he still needs to stay involved in terms of coaching and developing the team members.

The team is in its teenage years—it is beginning to blossom but not quite ready to make it on its own.

Here are the key phrases that helped us reach that conclusion:

"We're not quite ready to do it all on our own, so we still need help from Jen and others. But we are close."

"The majority of the team is able to lead at least one of our critical work activities, albeit still with some good periodic coaching from our manager, Heinz."

How do you view this example in relation to your team? Is your team at or near this stage? Why? What strategies would you apply to ensure that they keep going in the right direction? What help might you need?

By studying and understanding each of these examples, you will be able to identify where your team is currently, on the continuum of team development. You'll know where to look for both the warning signs and the opportunities, so you can then plan to take your team to the next level. The tools, techniques, and frameworks we provide in the remainder of this chapter will greatly assist you.

Another, more detailed way for you to gauge your team's development is through a set of descriptors. Descriptors are sometimes written to show what your team is currently doing and expected to do in the future in *each of your functional areas*. Descriptors can also be questions used to prompt your team members to look at where they are and how they need to grow. Here are three key questions to ask:

1. What do we need to know and how can we apply this knowledge to do this work?

2. What help do we need and where are we going to get that help?

3. What decisions are we going to be making and what information do we need to make those decisions?

Let's examine a list of possible descriptors for a manufacturing plant. Note that for the sake of simplicity, we have included only a limited number of functional categories. (Note, too, that the descriptors would be different for a white-collar activity.) For each function, there is also a person or point of contact responsible for the team development, as follows:

Team Development Descriptors

Function	Responsible for Team Development
1. Safety (and Environment)	Safety Focus Point
2. Scheduling	Value Delivery Focus Point
3. Inventory Management	Value Delivery Focus Point
4. Quality	Quality Focus Point
5. Financial Management	Wealth Creation Focus Point
6. Team Performance Management	Focus Manager

The actual and full descriptions for the manufacturing plant are shown in Figure 1-4. The approach we take in this illustration is to have each team member indicate in the right-hand column of the descriptor list (with a tick or a cross) where they believe the behavior of their team is *80 percent of the time.*

The information provided by the team members will indicate the team's progress in each of the functional areas. It will also help estimate the development stage of the team and allow the team to compare its results to other teams. Finally, these team development descriptors will provide the team and management with crucial information that will enable them to formulate a plan to take the team to the next level(s) in each function.

It should be noted that no team is perfect in every area; the world simply doesn't work that way. Accordingly, you should not expect your team to be at Stage Five in every one of the team's functions and activities. However, we strongly encourage you to *strive* toward Stage Five in each and every area.

FIGURE 1-4. Team development descriptors.

Safety (and Environment)

Stage of Development	Development Descriptor	Rating
I	Team members understand unsafe acts and correct safety norms; however, they rely on the Focus Manager to confront unsafe behavior. Accident and incident investigation is carried out by the Focus Manager.	
II	Team members understand and generally observe behavioral norms. Some team members address unsafe behaviors (unsafe acts), although there is still a strong dependence on the Focus Manager to communicate standards and address unsafe behaviour. The Safety Focus Point in the team starts to investigate accidents and incidents. However, this point still requires help from the Focus Manager when developing and implementing corrective actions.	
III	The Safety Focus Point begins to share with the Focus Manager the leadership responsibility within the team for safety management. Team members regularly address unsafe behaviors (acts) and have a clear understanding of the behavioral norms. They investigate accidents and incidents and have the Focus Manager facilitate the team reviews of results and corrective actions. The team starts to conduct certain studies and audits within its own boundaries, although the Focus Manager and Safety Focus Point still help with interpreting data and assigning priorities. The Focus Manager helps primarily with issues across team and shift boundaries.	
IV	The Safety Focus Point provides the primary leadership to the team in safety management. Team members review accidents and incidents effectively. They assign priorities, implement corrective actions, and review results. They conduct their own studies and take corrective action (they fix hazards identified and make equipment and procedural modifications). They analyze to identify improvement opportunities. They participate in continuous improvement efforts to make the facility injury-free. They begin to analyze the safety trends (near miss, unsafe acts, and equipment reports) to look for improvement opportunities, such as injury reduction across team and shift boundaries. With the assistance of the Focus Manager, the team begins to engage external resources, such as safety suppliers and experts, in improving the safety management of the whole conversion process.	
V	Team asks, "What could be unsafe?" Team members invent new ways to eliminate and prevent incidents. They help each other by conducting audits outside their team boundaries and benchmark outside the facility. They understand and seek out best safety practices from many sources. They help other teams to learn and apply safety management techniques. They consider the safety implications of the use of the product or process and make adjustments as necessary. They seek advice from many sources and invite input from auditing, so as to acquire the most recent and innovative safety management knowledge. Team members actively and voluntarily participate in communities of practice to increase their safety knowledge.	

FIGURE 1-4. Team development descriptors. *(continued)*

Scheduling

Stage of Development	Development Descriptor	Rating
I	Team members rely on the Focus Manager to schedule production runs, planned maintenance activities, holidays, breaks, lunches, housekeeping, overtime, training, meetings, contract labor, and team member hours. Focus Manager interacts primarily one-on-one with team members. Team members provide input on individual scheduling needs to Focus Manager. Team members are primarily focused on individual activities and tasks, and they have technical competence in a few areas.	
II	Team members provide input on planned maintenance, contract labor, and team member hours. Team members spend some time with each other discussing these scheduling items, but this is clearly under the direction of the Focus Manager. The Focus Manager leads the team in these decision-making processes. Team members begin to learn additional technical and administrative tasks.	
III	Team members schedule holidays, additional hours, learning programs, breaks, lunches, housekeeping, training, meetings, contract labor, and team member hours with guidance and facilitation from their Focus Manager. They also provide input and begin making local decisions on production run scheduling and planned maintenance activities but rely primarily on the Focus Manager's assistance in these areas, particularly in resolving problems and clarifying priorities. The Value Delivery Focus Point begins to take primary leadership responsibility within the team for the scheduling.	
IV	Team members schedule annual leave days, additional production hours, learning programs, planned maintenance activities, breaks, lunches, housekeeping, training, meetings, contract labor, and team member hours without help. They are involved in, and provide input to, broader scheduling meetings. They communicate scheduling needs and conflicts across teams and shifts and begin to participate in plantwide local scheduling decisions. The Value Delivery Focus Point provides the primary leadership to the team in scheduling. The Focus Manager coordinates and facilitates scheduling activities with sister plants.	
V	Team members invent new ways to meet the scheduling needs of the business and the individual team members. Team members create schedules and a scheduling process that is flexible and enables them to respond to changing business requirements. They communicate with and between shifts, teams, and sister plants in order to facilitate additional flexibility and responsiveness. They seek and understand scheduling best practices from many sources in order to provide innovative scheduling solutions. Team members actively participate in communities of practice to increase their scheduling knowledge.	

continue

FIGURE 1-4. Team development descriptors. *(continued)*

Inventory Management

Stage of Development	Development Descriptor	Rating
I	Team members understand the basics of inventory management through either one-on-one meetings or team meetings with the Focus Manager. They take responsibility for inventory management of their respective areas of work. They interact with the Focus Manager one-on-one, getting instructions or assignments and sometimes providing ideas, status updates, or input into decisions. Team members rely on the Focus Manager to work with them to ensure that inventory items (such as raw materials, production and maintenance supplies, and finished and unfinished goods) are correct.	
II	Team members begin to interact with each other around inventory management work, but they continue to be led by the Focus Manager on performance objectives, priorities, and problem-solving activities. For example, the Focus Manager shows team members how to investigate discrepancies. Team members begin to apply knowledge and take action to prevent discrepancies. The team understands and begins to use inventory management tools and techniques such as kanban and JIT to meet performance objectives.	
III	The Value Delivery Focus Point begins to share with the Focus Manager the leadership responsibility within the team for inventory management. Teams track and review inventory on a regular basis as a team. The team applies inventory management tools such as kanban and JIT to improve its performance. The Focus Manager and Value Delivery Focus Point help the team decide on how best to ensure the timeliness and accuracy of inventory numbers. The team investigates discrepancies and corrects inventories, often with help from the Focus Manager and Value Delivery Focus Point. The Focus Manager helps primarily with issues across team and shift boundaries.	
IV	The Value Delivery Focus Point provides the primary leadership to the team in inventory management. Team members schedule and conduct inventory reviews. They spend little time on discrepancy corrective action as they have developed accurate and timely tracking measures. They begin to analyze the inventory trends to look for improvement opportunities, such as cost reduction across team and shift boundaries. They consistently apply inventory tools such as kanban and JIT to improve inventory cost. With the assistance of the Focus Manager, the team begins to engage external resources, such as suppliers and distributors, in improving inventory management for the whole value delivery system.	
V	The team invents new ways to reduce inventories. It explores opportunities across shift, team, and facility boundaries. The team seeks out best practices and applies them to the facility. They help other groups learn and apply the inventory management techniques they have used to consistently improve their inventory management performance. The team actively participates in communities of practice to assist in improving inventory management knowledge.	

FIGURE 1-4. Team development descriptors. *(continued)*

Quality

Stage of Development	Development Descriptor	Rating
I	Team members understand variances, but mostly interact, one-on-one, with the Focus Manager on these issues. The team understands quality objectives and uses basic quality tools effectively. Cause of quality reject is investigated by individual team members and reviewed with the Focus Manager. Team members provide input on improvement ideas and decisions to the Focus Manager.	
II	Team members develop skills to carry out basic quality control tests. They understand and help develop quality standards and operating procedures. Teams participate in more extensive quality training (SPC, ISO, etc.). The Focus Manager communicates quality deviations to the team and leads the team in corrective action, although team members begin to interact with each other on their variances and corrections.	
III	The Quality Focus Point team member begins to share with the Focus Manager the leadership responsibility within the team for quality. Team members achieve consistent quality requirements without intervention by the Focus Manager. They complete all required quality documentation and begin, with the facilitation of the Quality Focus Point and Focus Manager, to conduct audits to identify quality system improvements. They identify and are aware of the lost opportunity created by variances but require help from the Focus Manager and Quality Focus Point to analyze data. The team starts to prioritize and implement corrective actions and follows up most of the time. The team starts to appreciate and apply simple statistical process control and problem-solving tools. However, the team members periodically need the facilitation of the Focus Manager to use the tools they already know and to see the consequences of the different ideas they have. They lead discussions and decisions on improvements.	
IV	The team is responsible for its own quality and ensures that quality standards are met. Team members improve production procedures to optimize product quality. They develop continuous improvement plans with outside resources. The focus for improvement is on the whole system, with particular attention to upstream and downstream variations. The team is able to identify problem areas, apply problem-solving tools and techniques, create and implement corrective actions. They understand their process capability for each product and start to liaise (e.g., conduct audits, interviews) across team and shift boundaries to improve quality. The team develops continuous improvement plans; the Focus Manager acts as a resource when required; and the Quality Focus Point provides the leadership in the area.	
V	Team members can manage quality themselves. They set their own stretch goals and objectives and help other groups with their quality process and techniques to become self-managing. The team continuously improves on the process to prevent quality defects. Team members set their own goals and objectives by benchmarking across team, shift, and facility boundaries. The team innovates new ways to prevent variances and liaises directly with customers and suppliers to tap both articulated and unarticulated product and process quality needs. Team members seek advice from many sources to innovate quality performance. They seek and understand quality system best practices from many sources in order to provide innovative, value-adding process and product solutions for the customer. Team members actively participate in communities of practice to increase their quality system knowledge.	

continue

FIGURE 1-4. Team development descriptors. *(continued)*

Financial Management

Stage of Development	Development Descriptor	Rating
I	Team members understand the basics of financial management through either one-on-ones or team meetings with a Focus Manager. They understand the importance of financial management in running their team as a business. Team members will interact with the Focus Manager and provide budget or cost input to get their questions answered. Team members rely on the Focus Manager to develop budgets, explain cost of variances, and control spending and team costs. The team is aware of the wealth creation model but is reliant on the Focus Manager to do the calculation. The team relies on the Focus Manager to collect and report the team's key performance indicators (KPIs) vs. goals and objectives. The Focus Manager will report this information in a team meeting that the manager leads or in one-on-one sessions.	
II	Team members begin to interact with each other and provide input collectively and one-on-one to the Focus Manager. They understand the cause-and-effect relationship of their financials. They begin to calculate their own wealth model, investigate and explain cost of variances, and report KPI data. They still rely on the Focus Manager to lead the team by analyzing data, assigning priorities, and assisting in developing corrective action plans. The Focus Manager shows the team how the budget is developed and explains where help and input are required to be successful.	
III	The Wealth Creation Focus Point begins to take primary leadership for financial management within the team. Team members participate in budgeting, explaining variances, developing cost/benefit analysis, and developing information systems with both the Wealth Creation Focus Point and the Focus Manager's guidance. Team members monitor and control costs directly within their control and begin to look outside the team for opportunities for improvement. They often rely on the Wealth Creation Focus Point and the Focus Manager to help with priorities and help to follow up on corrective actions. They consistently report team KPI data and the current situation compared with budget.	
IV	The Wealth Creation Focus Point provides the leadership for financial management within the team. Team members have developed or can utilize systems to get information necessary to control costs, develop budgets, explain variances, and establish latest estimates (cash flow input). The Focus Manager assists the team as needed on more complex or challenging situations. The team plans ways to continuously improve costs and cost of variances so as to maximize the wealth generated, with the assistance of the Focus Manager. They start to explore opportunities across team shifts and facility boundaries.	
V	Teams control their costs, develop their own budgets, explain variances, and establish accurate forecasts. Teams develop capital applications for projects and share their knowledge openly with other teams in a community of practice that stretches beyond the boundaries of the facility. They seek knowledge from many different sources so as to innovate financial management solutions. They help these other teams apply the knowledge to improve their performance and the overall performance of the organization.	

FIGURE 1-4. Team development descriptors. *(continued)*

Team Performance Management

Stage of Development	Development Descriptor	Rating
I	Team members understand their team objectives and KPIs (cost, yield, OEE, safety, etc.) through one-on-ones and team meetings led by the Focus Manager. Team members provide input on improvement ideas and decisions to the Focus Manager. The Focus Manager reviews and interprets results and determines priorities and necessary actions and communicates these either at team meetings (which the manager leads) or in one-on-one meetings. The Focus Manager ensures follow-up on action items. Team members are primarily focused on individual activities and tasks and have technical competence in a few specialties.	
II	Team members understand their objectives and KPIs (cost, yield, OEE, safety, etc.) and regularly review their weekly results. The Focus Manager leads team performance review meetings and helps the team to better understand and interpret weekly results. Team members provide input and discuss results. They begin to take some responsibility to follow up with each other on action items. Team members begin to learn additional technical and administrative tasks.	
III	Team members are able to interpret and understand performance objectives and reports and understand why it is important to review them regularly. They run team performance review meetings. They identify gaps, establish action items, and follow up on action items; however, they rely on the Focus Manager's help to sort out the right priorities or follow up often on some action items. The team still depends on the team leader to help identify performance gaps (especially performance problems regarding coordinating with teams working other shifts) and to ensure that people assume accountability to follow up on action items. The team depends on the Focus Manager to help facilitate meetings to ensure that time is used effectively.	
IV	The team reviews the performance results effectively on a regular basis without support or facilitation of the Focus Manager. Team members set priorities and follow up on action items effectively and consistently. They use their time in results review sessions effectively: Participation and facilitation are shared. The team begins to focus a greater percentage of its resources on how its performance affects and is affected by other teams. Periodically, team members may need the Focus Manager's help in addressing cross-boundary issues successfully (across state change teams and shifts).	
V	The team consistently exceeds its KPI performance objectives. Team members consult with other teams to help them learn and review their performance results and to follow up on action items more effectively. They analyze trends in performance to enable them to do long-term planning, as well as short-term and weekly planning. They establish communities of practice for learning and sharing learning that transcend team, shift, and organizational boundaries. The team benchmarks comparable work groups in world-class manufacturing plants to set world-class performance objectives.	

STARTING UP AND DEVELOPING HIGH-PERFORMANCE TEAMS

We use four common tools as the cornerstones for accelerating the building of high-performing teams. They are:

1. The Team Development Model

2. Herrmann Brain Dominance Instrument (HBDI)

3. Team Communication

4. Team Startup

It is important that everyone have this same tool kit because it provides all team members with a common language and accelerates the diffusion of knowledge, which helps get people up to speed.

Let's examine each one of these tools in greater detail.

THE TEAM DEVELOPMENT MODEL

We have already discussed the model in some depth, so we will not repeat ourselves here. However, be aware that there are four factors that will affect your team's movement toward self-sufficiency. They are:

1. Maturity

2. Knowledge

3. Complexity

4. Fluidity

The more mature your team is, the more quickly it will evolve along the continuum of self-management. By the same token, the better a team is at diffusing knowledge, the faster it will assume higher-level tasks and achieve greater independence.

On the other hand, the more complexity your team has to deal with, the longer it will take for the team to become self-managing. More issues to deal with means, as a rule, more knowledge to assimilate and diffuse. At the same time, if the team is evolving within a situation that is highly fluid (because of political issues, leadership changes, budget concerns, market challenges, high turnover, etc.), it may need more time to move between stages since there will be a large number of adjustments for the team to make along the way.

Of course, the more advanced your team is at a particular stage, the easier it will be for the team to deal with these factors. After all, the more cross-trained the team members are, the better they will be at problem solving and the more flexible they will be in dealing with fluid situations. That is exactly why your team needs to be assessed—so it can tailor the development plan to the current situation.

HBDI

This instrument was developed by Ned Herrmann, the originator of Whole Brain Thinking and author of *The Whole Brain Business Book*. He first pioneered the study of the brain in the field of business while at GE.[1] The Herrmann Brain Dominance Instrument is an assessment that profiles an individual's preferred thinking style, which is extremely helpful when looking at the composition of your team. Figure 1-5 is an illustration of the Whole Brain Thinking Model.[2]

FIGURE 1-5. Whole Brain Thinking Model.

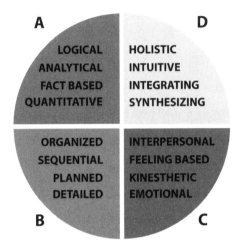

Source: The four-color, four quadrant graphic, Whole Brain Thinking® and HBDI®, are trademarks of Herrmann Global, © 2013.

The HBDI assessment is a tool, not a "test." It measures your team members' thinking/learning-style *preference(s),* not their skills or competence. By understanding people's thinking and learning preferences, and those of the people they work with, team members can increase the speed and success of their own learning and the learning of others. Thus, they can begin to recognize and therefore appreciate the mental diversity that people bring to your team. With this information, your team can:

- Increase its communication abilities
- Leverage what differences people bring to the table in order to develop a highly effective team
- Tap into creativity as a natural mental resource and learn how to build an environment in which creativity thrives

When your team has discovered its preferences using an HBDI team re-port, you will achieve a greater appreciation for how members of your team:

- Learn

- Communicate

- Make decisions

- Solve problems

- Perform when stressed under pressure

Armed with this knowledge, your team will:

- Accelerate learning within the team process

- Generate more creative, robust ideas

- Promote individual creativity

TEAM COMMUNICATION

It is good to be a Whole Brain team and appreciate it. Whole Brain teams can succeed wildly, but they can also fail miserably if they have difficulty communicating. These days, since the overwhelming majority of teams are heterogeneous, we are providing you with a tool that allows all your team members to be able to appreciate differences and communicate ef-fectively. We call it "team communication."

Team communication provides a framework for creating a common language for giving and receiving feedback around difficult topics to dis-cuss. In essence, it accelerates your team's learning and its ability to build skills in difficult areas.

When your team forms and begins its journey toward self-management, you will be faced with all sorts of difficult topics. For example, who is responsible for what? Many members initially feel uncomfortable asking these types of questions, as they don't want to rock the boat or step on someone else's toes. Others may quickly conclude that a team environment is not meeting their expectations, yet they may not want to raise the issue out of fear they will be labeled "a troublemaker," "a whiner," or "not a team player."

Another challenging issue involves interpersonal conflicts—that is, when two or more people have a personality conflict, it may be cultural in nature or simply due to the fact that they see things very differently. Perhaps one has a strong personality and is very loud and demanding whereas another person is quieter and more laid-back. Maybe two individuals have different work ethics. Or you may simply have team members who disagree on the path going forward and after a while the disagreement becomes personal.

Finally, perhaps the most difficult issue for your team will occur when one or more members have a performance problem or misbehave. Since your team is probably used to the team leader handling these types of difficult issues, they are often ill prepared to deal with them as a team.

That is why we recommend that you invest in a common model for team communication and learn together how to use it—because it will provide your team members with the skills necessary to communicate and deal with difficult issues. This very simple but effective communication model involves:

- *Obtaining value by seeking input from others—skillfully.* Team members are taught to be open-minded, which entails asking others for their viewpoints and ideas and asking others to challenge your ideas and viewpoint.

- *Listening with the intent to understand.* The objective here is to capture information before you expand on, judge, and/or evaluate an idea.

- *Giving your input skillfully and respectfully.* The skill involves using phrases that are not inflammatory, such as "It seems" or "I believe," so you can get your point across and have it received unemotionally.

Mastering these types of "crucial conversations"[3] within a new or developing team will go a long way toward bringing everyone together. It will help your team's members learn the importance and power of dialogue, teach them how to truly listen, and show them how to transform what are often emotional conversations into positive interactions that will benefit each member and the team itself.

It will also help build trust among people, which is always important to any team. *The Speed of Trust: The One Thing That Changes Everything*[4] makes the point that trust is perhaps the most important ingredient for any high-performance, successful team/organization. Straight talk accompanied by mutual respect, transparency, and appropriate action will clearly result in increased trust within your team.

TEAM STARTUP

The "team startup" tool kit is not only useful for when your team first forms; it's also intended to be used as often as needed. These tools are based on the twin objectives of developing your team from the beginning but also intervening when appropriate.

From the start, your team will need an enormous amount of development. However, down the road, if the team dynamic changes in some way, or if other issues crop up, it would also be a good idea to revisit some of the tools. For example, if your team has added new members, it would be a good time to revisit these tools.

There are a variety of tools that can be used and steps that can be taken to support your team's startup, but they all focus on four areas:

1. Goals (performance agreements)

2. Roles

3. Processes/procedures

4. People development/relationships

We focus on these areas because we want to accomplish three primary objectives in the startup phase: 1) clarifying expectations, 2) minimizing frustration, and 3) getting teams focused.

Bill Dyer,[5] who was called the "father of team building," stated that whenever he saw frustration in a group it was almost always a result of a violation of expectations. The cause of the violation of expectations was usually due to a lack of clarity around expectations. Research states that most expectations are usually implicit rather than explicit. As a result, the tools we are about to describe are designed to make expectations within your team explicit and thereby reduce frustrations.

Additionally, the people within your team only bring so much energy to the workplace; if you are being clear about expectations, it is more likely they will focus their energy in a positive rather than a negative direction.

Here, then, are brief descriptions of the actual tools that will help your team start off on the right foot. Note that these tools/elements are tightly interlinked, which should always be the case when making design choices.

Performance agreements. This is where your team agrees on the goals and objectives it intends to achieve (initially at the team level and eventually down to the individual level). Desired performance is what should drive all other discussions. For example, what type of culture does your team need in order to hit its targets? What knowledge must be shared? As long as your team knows what is expected of it, people will be able to focus their energy in a positive manner.

Defined norms and roles. For an effective launch, your team must invest some time to get organized. That is because a well-organized team has 1) a clear charter outlining its purpose, guiding principles, scope, and team membership; 2) agreed-on norms of behavior (e.g., treat each other with respect, be on time, listen, respect confidentiality); and 3) clear roles/responsibilities in regards to tasks and processes, communication, record keeping, and facilitating and scheduling meetings.

Decision-making process. Successful teams employ one or both forms of decision making: 1) consensus and/or 2) majority vote. Under consensus, everyone agrees with and is in full support of the decision. Using a majority vote, everyone agrees to support the decision agreed to by the majority.

Here is our recommended decision-making process:

- Clarify and agree on what your team is deciding: What is the decision to be made?

- Have open, honest dialogue in regard to pertinent issues, points of view, and alternatives.

- When all points of view are in, and your members feel understood and comprehend the decision they are making, have everyone agree to the form of decision (i.e., consensus or majority vote).

- Poll the group.

- Reaffirm the decision and each team member's support.

- Document the decision.

Assimilation plan. This is a plan that helps your team members get up to speed and contribute as quickly as possible. To put this plan together and successfully implement it, your team has to come together to support new members while ensuring there isn't a dip in overall team performance. As part of the process, your team may choose to have social/team and technical/expertise mentors. These mentors will need to share the team development tools and learnings with the new team member.

Value creation and sizing model. During startup you need to incorporate the team value creation model (discussed further in Chapter 4) along with a simple model that determines the number of people needed by your team to do its core work. For example, if your team were responsible for answering customer calls, the model would show the number of calls the team expects to receive (based on past experience and future projections) and the number of people the team would need to handle them. These tools provide your team members with a framework for determining what is required to achieve the value they need to contribute as a team and also help your team make better decisions about what new knowledge needs to be gained or shared to increase the value the team can create.

Planned people movement. The idea of "planned" movement is that movement does not hurt your team. With planned movement, individuals are clear about what they need to do before moving to a new position. As people move from team to team, they will share the common language of the team development framework, which will help them get up to speed faster, thus causing less downtime for your team to achieve its goals.

Communities of practice (CoP). "Communities of practice are groups of people who share a concern or a passion for something they do and learn how to do it better as they interact regularly."[6] They are all about knowledge sharing and helping to build relationships. CoPs are formed around critical knowledge domains across the organization. Your team will be better prepared to take on support functions by joining CoPs around their support function, thus moving your team through the stages of the Five-Stage Team Development Model.[7]

Career development. By being a part of an organization that focuses on sharing and diffusing knowledge, your team's members become more marketable not only within their own sector, but outside it. Naturally, besides helping each employee individually, a process that creates better-developed team members will also benefit your team.

Customer value added (CVA) score. This is a tool that helps your team focus on and determine the value it provides to your customers. It measures the satisfaction of a team's customers *relative to its competitors.* The tool uses the premise that customers decide to purchase products/services based on their perception of value. "Customer value" is "the quality you get for the price you pay."[8]

The key question for your team to ask its customers is, "Considering the products/services offered, how would you rate their worth relative to what you paid for them?" This "worth what paid for" question is often abbreviated WWPF.

The CVA score is the ratio of the team's WWPF score relative to the score of the competition, so:

$$\text{CVA} \quad = \frac{\text{WWPF for the team}}{\text{WWPF for competitors}}$$

A NOTE ABOUT THE IMPACT OF TEAMS ON FAMILIES

As we've already mentioned, this book (and this chapter) apply to a variety of team-based settings, including a family. After all, most families operate as some form of a team.

Families also operate at different stages of development. For example, a single-parent family with relatively few options and many challenges (financial constraints, limited education, drugs, teenage pregnancy) is more likely to operate at Stage One or Stage Two. Of course, problems are not limited to single-parent families, as those with two parents can have just as many, if not more, problems. Constant bickering among the parents, alcoholism, job loss, one or more affairs, and any number of issues may cause these problems. In many cases, the problems are not dramatic and are simply caused by a lack of family/team skills.

By contrast, a well-established family, whether it centers around one or two parents, tends to be at a higher stage of development. Most likely, these families have greater access to resources, more community ties, and clearer roles and responsibilities. They probably have strong values that help unite the family around a common set of core beliefs. Finally, they usually have effective role models that have been willing to pass on their expertise to the next generation.

All families often unite against adversity (e.g., problems with a neighbor, death of a loved one, job loss). However, once the adversity goes away, the same problems almost always reappear. That is because adversity tends to mask the root causes of a family's problems but almost never solves them. They simply go on the back burner during the period of adversity—*but they are still real and still there.*

Without the requisite structure and accompanying tools, they are going to repeat the mistakes of the past and, of course, continue to have the same types of problems.

Let's look at a couple of real-life examples of families who are very familiar with our principles, tools, and techniques and have used them to improve their group dynamics and overall teamwork.

In one of the families, the approach to family vacations evolved significantly over time. They started at Stage One, with one of the parents telling each family member what the plans were for their vacation. They evolved to Stage Two when the parent began to talk it over with the children and ask for their ideas for the family vacation. As they moved to Stage Three, one or two of the family members stepped up and planned a part of the family vacation.

By Stage Four, most of the family members had planned a part of the vacation. Finally, at Stage Five, when the family decided to go to Europe, all the children chose a country and planned out the activities they would do in that country, with just a cursory review by one of the parents. It should be noted that Stage Five is more likely to occur in a mature family, with the children at or near college age and having the skill sets to plan out all the activities.

Another family had two key family events each year—the Passover and Thanksgiving dinners. Because it was a blended family, initially there were plenty of challenges in terms of roles and responsibilities, different perspectives, and jealousy. The first dinner was clearly a Stage One event, with virtually all the planning, shopping, cooking, serving, and cleaning being done by the parents. They eventually moved on to Stage Two, when a couple of kids offered suggestions on how to improve the dinner and overall experience. After that, in Stage Three, several kids helped out by preparing some side dishes and assisting with the cleanup.

By Stage Four, most of the kids were now involved—one designed the table settings and overall staging; several others became heavily involved with the cooking and cleaning, while others planned the activities (games, watching videos) for the gathering after the meal was over. These days, they are at Stage Five, as everyone is now involved and several different family members have offered to host these meals.

Neither of the families in our examples moved through the stages by magic. In fact, both of the leaders of these families were well versed on the Five-Stage Team Development Model, although at the beginning they primarily used it at work. However, they both grasped its importance and applicability to their home environments and used the tools described herein to take their families to a better place.

Ultimately, both families developed a clearer sense of purpose—a value-creating purpose—with informal norms of behavior and a communication plan (through group discussions, one-on-one talks, and even text messages where necessary). They were able to develop their families because they nurtured them in the same way they would have helped to develop work teams.

CHALLENGES, TENSIONS, AND KEY FACTORS DURING IMPLEMENTATION

Perhaps the greatest challenge to implementing the Five-Stage Team Development Model will be the initial lack of knowledge and support of the concept within your team. Expect your supervisor to be skeptical of the idea and resistant to giving up some of the power he currently possesses. Don't be surprised if at least some of your coworkers are also dubious of the approach. Some people will think it sounds too good to be true, while others may not wish to learn more, assume additional power, or become a leader.

The best way to address these concerns is through education. Give everyone a copy of this book. Visit other organizations that have self-managed teams. Have senior managers explain to the team why they plan to implement the concept and how it will be good for the organization, the team, and each employee. This would be a good time to describe the results expected once the concept has been fully implemented.

For those that are still resistant, let them know that participation is mandatory, not optional. If they still do not want to be part of the team, advise them that the train has already left the station. If they do not want to get on board, inform them that it is time to move on, and, if possible, offer to help them find another job.

It is also important to invite and answer questions from everyone in a variety of forums (e.g., town hall meetings, group discussions, one-on-one sessions, written queries) so that as many issues as possible are brought forth and addressed. After all, the more concerns that are addressed early on, the easier the implementation will be. In addition, the more people learn about the concept and how it will evolve, including its proven benefits, the more supportive they will become.

Recognize that converting, embracing, and implementing a philosophy of self-directed teams is not an easy thing to do; it requires hard work and careful planning. Let people know this reality, so they will understand what to expect. Include both champions and skeptics in the planning and implementation phases so that they will take ownership of the changes being made. Finally, use the many tools that we will provide you in the next five chapters to help make your journey as smooth and effective as possible.

Having been in lots of teams over our lifetimes in many environments—work, church, sports, family, community, not-for-profit, communities of practice—we assure you that the personal energy that comes from moving up the continuum of the five-stage model is exhilarating and rewarding, both as an individual team member and as a leader of such a high-performing team.

HOW USING THE FIVE-STAGE TEAM DEVELOPMENT MODEL WILL HELP BUILD LEADERS

For a team to reach the final stage of development, every member of the team will have to become a leader. Many of the strategies, tools, and techniques outlined in this book are designed to accomplish just that. So, you might say that for teams that properly use the model, building leaders will become a self-fulfilling prophecy.

Secrets of Great Design

***Key principle:** For everyone to become a leader, the team's management systems and design choices must be designed, aligned, and properly implemented.*

WE'VE TALKED ABOUT THE importance of self-managed teams and the evolution your team must go through to eventually reach Stage Five. Now let's discuss how you can actually get there.

"Teams are perfectly designed to get the results that they get." This principle is the starting place for designing your team. Simply put, if for any reason your team wants different results from what it is now getting, you will have to change your design.

For example, if your results are showing a gap between current and envisioned performance, or if you simply aspire to be better than you are now, you will need to redesign your team to get different results. Framed differently, if your teammates are acting like followers rather than leaders, look at your design.

To begin, you will want to size up your structure and management systems and adjust them so that they align with your overall strategy. You will have to make choices so that your goals, workflows, structures, decision-making practices, and other routines fit together to uniformly drive you toward the same result. Along the way, you will have to watch carefully for incongruent policies or initiatives that may have a sabotaging effect on other elements in your system.

The most successful high-performing teams have a common vision and purpose, and the degree to which you can involve your people in the cause, and help them become strongly connected to one another, is what will electrify and unify your team and help everyone realize its greatest hopes for success.

CONNECTING TEAM MEMBERS AROUND A SENSE OF PURPOSE

Before we delve into team design, it is important to discuss the concept of uniting your team around a purpose. Nobody jumps out of bed and runs to work and says, "Thank goodness I work for a cost center." Nobody starts off the day by saying, "I can't wait to make more money for the shareholder." People are simply not wired that way.

Human beings want to have a sense of purpose: We want to believe the lives we lead and the work we do has meaning. Otherwise, what is the point of our lives and the work we do?

People come to work with energy, wanting to do the right thing. When you are clear on your mission and see how your efforts can make a positive impact, you will enthusiastically go forward, trying to both lead and accomplish your goals and objectives.

Conversely, if you don't find any meaning in what you do, or if you believe you are working for an unfair and/or hypocritical team, you will eventually become cynical and/or channel your energy in a negative way, whether it is deluding management into believing you are doing a good job, filing grievances and complaints, or simply slowing down and calling in sick.

The point here is that when team members in virtually any forum believe their work has meaning and is connected to a higher purpose, incredible things tend to happen. New and often breakthrough products get built in record time; productivity dramatically increases; quality improves; customer satisfaction goes way up; profits soar. Any team design/redesign project should always keep this principle in mind.

YOU GET WHAT YOU DESIGN FOR

If your team's results are disappointing, the explanation lies in an understanding of your infrastructure: your strategies and systems and your derivative culture. And the good news is that's where the remedy lies as well, because the way your team works can be changed. You can overhaul the rules you have put in place about how to do things. You can change procedures, remodel, rework, restore, revamp, and reconnect.

By making thoughtful choices about team design and adjusting design elements where possible—like the goals and principles that provide guidance, work activities and facilities, decision-making processes, approaches to recruiting and training and rewarding and learning—your team can remake itself systematically and develop an environment where everyone becomes a leader.

Figure 2-1 is the Organization Systems Design (OSD) Model adapted for Teams, by Paul Gustavson. This model illustrates the components of a team working together and shows their combined impact on results.

Looking at the model, we visualize team performance on the right-hand side of the chart—the "outcomes" oval. Outcomes are the result of all the choices your team makes—choices about strategy as well as systems and structures, as depicted by the large middle rectangle. The ex-

FIGURE 2-1. OSD Model for Teams.

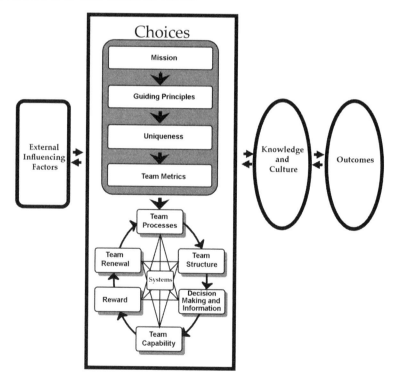

ternal environment, represented by the left-hand box, inevitably affects (and is affected by) your team as well. Your team's culture—shown in Figure 2-1 as the oval on the left—is hugely shaped by all your team's choices and can have a filtering or focusing effect, diluting or turbocharging final performance.

The model provides a framework for understanding the relationships that affect your team's outcomes—relationships between your external environment, design choices, culture, and outcomes. Teams generally exist at a variety of levels within most organizations. In fact, the team-level model in Figure 2-1 shows the same basic framework, relationships, and outcomes that occur at every level of an organization.

For your team to reach Stage Five of the team development model and produce the highest level of performance, all the requisite design elements should be in place.

Before we go forward, let's discuss the concept of alignment. Alignment is the way your team's elements fit together. For example, if your team truly values quality, it cannot focus merely on its methods (i.e., information systems) for measuring product quality. Your team must also give thought to what guiding principles will be shared about quality, what strategies will best drive quality, what tasks and technologies make quality achievable, what structure will be needed to implement those strategies, what competencies are needed to produce a quality product, what rewards will best compensate behavior aimed at quality, and what continuous improvement approach will be deployed. This is the holistic view that must be applied to your team: Changes in one aspect will necessitate—and may unavoidably generate—change throughout the systems that govern the team.

Let's look at a real-world example of this type of situation. An organization we worked with kept announcing that quality work was a high priority. However, behind the scenes, all it emphasized was productivity, productivity, and productivity. Along the way, little effort was placed on establishing support systems to drive quality. While the goals reflected output, timeliness, and quality, at every management meeting, the bulk of the discussions revolved around the number of actions completed. Naturally, the employees in the subordinate teams took the message that the only thing that really mattered was productivity.

At the end of the year, large bonuses were given to the best-performing teams. One series of teams, which received a substantial bonus, had high productivity but also the second lowest quality out of all that organization's teams nationwide. From the employees' perspective, this simply reinforced their suspicion that all management cared about was productivity and not quality.

From senior management's perspective, it realized a mistake had been made and vowed to ensure that all the organization's design elements would be aligned in future years. The problem, however, was that the managers had lost trust with the workforce, and it took years for them to recover from this debacle.

Getting back to the OSD Model for Teams, let's look at it more closely and examine all its elements. Then, after we discuss the model's components, we will explain how to apply the model.

The model (see Figure 2-1) shows that teams are open systems: They exist in an external environment from which they take inputs and convert them into outputs. You should consider all these elements within this context.

You begin with the left-hand side of the model because team design starts by understanding how all the elements of your team relate to each other. The first element on the left is *external influencing factors.*

The external environment places a constantly changing set of demands on your team, and you must learn to proactively respond to these requirements in order to survive. Of course, adaptation is not enough. Especially in a world where the global economy can gyrate, your team must learn how to influence the environment, at least within the context of your larger organization.

You may want to offer your customers exceptional service that they have never requested but that delights them once they see it; your suppliers may be willing to collaborate with you on technology solutions; and/ or you may help develop a creative strategy that can distinguish your team from others. All three examples show that your team can influence external expectations rather than take them as given.

There are five groups in your external environment:

1. Customers (both current and potential markets)

2. Stakeholders (shareowners and their representatives)

3. Influencers (suppliers, regulators, legislators)

4. Competitors

5. Best-in-class teams

Make sure you are well aware of all five of these groups and understand their needs and expectations. Then figure out how you can best influence them.

The next element we consider in the OSD Model for Teams, jumping to the right-hand side of Figure 2-1, is *outcomes*. As we have discussed, teams are perfectly designed to get the results that they get. Therefore, it is crucial to consider what outcomes you really desire before making any design choices.

There are five categories of potential outcomes, along with possible indicators for an organization. Let's review them.

Customer Indicators

- Customer satisfaction relative to your competitors
- Repeat buyer rate
- Customer referral rate
- Market share

Stakeholder Indicators

- Profit and loss
- Earnings growth and revenue
- Return on investment and equity

Community Indicators

- Sustainability practices
- Community perception survey scores
- Compliance ratings
- Public service awards

Operational Excellence Indicators

- Cycle times

- Quality results and ratings

- Quantity of units produced

- Commitments made to plan

- Plans developed and approved

Team "Voice of the Workforce" (VOWF) Indicators

- Turnover

- Safety record

- VOWF team survey scores

- Individual contribution to community (e.g., school boards, service organizations)

The actual indicators/metrics you choose for your team to some extent will reflect the size and focus of your team as well as its direct contribution to these organizational outcomes. Teams, for example, would relate their desired outcomes and align them to the organization's desired outcomes. A team's outcomes in the five categories—customer, stakeholder, community, operational excellence, and VOWF—might look something like this:

Customer

- Net promoter score

- Guest or customer relative experience and value score

Stakeholder (Financial)

- Cost per unit

- Value creation metric

Community

- Community service recognition

Operational Excellence

- Cycle time metric

- Customer schedule commitments that are met

Voice of the Workforce (VOWF)

- VOWF scores (i.e., engagement score or correlation to performance score)

- Turnover

- Capabilities developed

Now we come to *knowledge and culture*. Culture is "the way things get done around here." It is the set of shared basic assumptions or emotionally charged beliefs that develop over time among your team's members. It is manifested in symbols, stories, rituals, routines, and behavioral norms.

Your team's ability to learn, share, and apply new knowledge is the most important source of your competitive advantage. The culture of the team is a critical factor in its learning capability. Culture cannot be mandated, but it can be influenced. It modulates between design choices and outcomes—in other words, the explicit design choices you make will lead to improved results, but only through the culture of your team.

With respect to knowledge, your team should determine the knowledge that is its *competitive advantage,* including what is needed to be able to move up to Stage Five. It should then nurture its ability to capture and share new knowledge when it comes and then find ways to manage it; in other words, you want to ensure you develop, capture, share, and put the knowledge to wise use. Additional information on developing and managing your team's knowledge can be found in Chapter 5.

Concerning culture, it encompasses the behaviors, feelings, and values shared by your team's members. The effect on your culture will be positive when your team harmonizes its plans and processes and when your team members are brought together with a common purpose.

Now we come to *choices,* which we can subdivide into choices about your *strategy* and choices about your team's *systems.*

Regarding strategy, there are four types of choices for your team to make:

1. *Mission.* A mission statement identifies your primary reason for being and your distinctive competency. A good mission statement should be energizing, simple, and concise.

2. *Guiding principles.* These statements describe your team's underlying beliefs about the best way to create the right team culture to do business and achieve your mission and outcomes. They include beliefs that govern how teammates should treat

one another, as well as beliefs that should govern the decisions about the team's design choices.

3. *Uniqueness.* This is what separates your team from others and makes it special. In essence, it is your team's identity.

4. *Team metrics.* These are measures important for achieving your desired outcomes. They can be summarized as a set of key performance indicators that measure ongoing performance in four areas: 1) customer performance, 2) financial performance, 3) internal operating performance, and 4) culture and knowledge.

Your team cannot make the overall strategic choices for your organization. That is the role of the organization's leaders. They need to be closely aligned with the organization's strategy, which will have a direct impact on your team's future. Moreover, you can and should make supplemental choices at the team level (e.g., the team's mission in supporting the organization; additional guiding principles such as "we have each others' backs"; team-level strategies to work with members of their environment; additional internal team goals). The key here is that your team must stay consistent with the organization's strategy while exercising its own initiative to excel.

When we discuss choices about your team's systems, we identify six categories of systems in every team (as shown in Figure 2-1):

1. *The team's business processes* deal with the activities you routinely carry out to create and deliver value for your customers. It also encompasses your physical arrangements for interacting and exchanging knowledge and technology.

2. *The structural system* is the way your team is organized.

3. *The decision-making and information system* deals with decision-making processes throughout your team. What specific responsibilities are given to which roles? What are your planning processes? What are your critical decisions and how are they made? It also includes choices about the capture, distribution, and display of information. A RACI (responsible, approves, consulted, informed) chart is a good tool to use in the decision-making process.

4. *The people system* pertains to how people are attracted, selected, oriented, trained, certified, performance managed, and promoted. It includes capability and career development choices.

5. *The reward system* is your pay and benefits structure; it also includes incentives, celebrations, and informal rewards and recognitions.

6. *The renewal system* is the way you encourage and formalize continuous learning process and performance improvement. What structures or processes are in place for gathering together to learn, to share best practices, and improve team processes and performance? When a problem-solving discussion takes place in an individual or team review, how do employees put the ideas generated into practice? How do they report back on the results? How are things updated?

USING THE OSD MODEL FOR
TEAMS TO REVIEW YOUR CHOICES

Given what we have just explained, this would be a good time to review your own team's current/future design choices. Along these lines, Figure 2-2 is a blank OSD Model for Teams in which you can write your observations about design choices in your team.

Ask yourself, what are your external influencing factors? What is your team's mission? What are your guiding principles, strategies, and goals? What is the design of your systems? What behaviors do you see,

FIGURE 2-2. OSD Model for Teams: Fill in the blanks with your design choices.

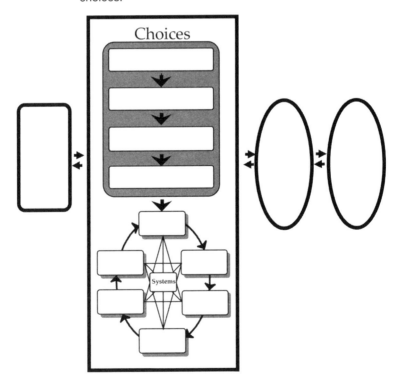

and how do you feel about them? What results does your team get? Once again, as you look at the model, also ask yourself how consistent these elements are in supporting the organization's overall strategy.

If you start to look at your team in this light, when problems develop you will become less likely to blame someone for them and more likely to find your answer embedded within weaknesses in your system.

DESIGN GUIDELINES

If you decide that a redesign effort is required, it is helpful to have some guidelines to follow. Design guidelines not only provide boundaries for your team, but also serve as principles to aid you in decision making.

Let's outline some sample design guidelines.

MISSION

A mission statement will identify our primary reason for being. It will be energizing, simple, concise, and supportive of the overall organization's mission.

OUTCOMES

We agree to measure ourselves against the following criteria:

- Our products and services completely satisfy our customers' expectations so that relative customer satisfaction ratios exceed 1.05. The number of annual safety recordables does not exceed three.

- Return on investment is 15 percent.
- Legislators, regulators, and the public view us as a valuable member of the community.

CULTURE AND KNOWLEDGE

People here are dedicated to:

- Sharing the mission and goals
- Living the values
- Demonstrating openness and honesty and trusting others
- Providing good leadership
- Having technical competence
- Taking risks to make the vision a reality
- Being accountable for their own actions
- Being multiskilled and flexible

GUIDING PRINCIPLES

To support the aforementioned behaviors, feelings, and attributes, we adopt the following guiding principles:

- Having the necessary resources, training, and feedback enables us to meet customer needs.
- Being technically competent is a prerequisite for overall quality and customer satisfaction.
- Being empowered motivates us to become leaders, take initiative, and engage in continuous improvement.

- Having respectful leadership makes us feel trusted and minimizes the fear of failure.

- Having shared goals encourages us to work as a team. We have each others' backs.

STRATEGY

Within the context of the overall organization's strategy, our primary strategy is to perform activities that are different from our competitors, or to perform the same activities differently.

GOALS AND OBJECTIVES

- All goals and objectives support our mission, guiding principles, and desired outcomes.

- All goals and objectives are attainable (realistic), challenging, measurable, understandable, and clearly communicated.

- Our people can see how their work relates to their goals and will act as leaders in order to achieve them.

BUSINESS PROCESSES

- Jobs are designed to be meaningful.

- People have the information and tools they need to do their jobs.

- Systems or tasks that do not add value are eliminated.

- Variances are controlled at the source.

TECHNOLOGIES

- Systems do what they were designed to do, are economically flexible, and are cost-effective.

- Systems design recognizes opportunities for synergy across the team and organization.

- An understanding of what technology can do is embedded in all design decisions.

FACILITIES

- Workspace and workstations are consistent with the needs of the job.

- The work environment is clean, efficient, inviting, inspiring, and conducive to learning.

- Physical arrangements (to the extent possible) bring people in contact with others when they need to work together to meet customer requirements.

- Visual management is used as a competitive advantage and to reinforce everything we are trying to accomplish. (See Chapter 6 for a complete description of visual management.)

STRUCTURE

- Boundaries minimize the transfer of variances and promote effectiveness and communication. It is easy for groups who need to work together to do so.

- Fewer levels and wider spans of control permit decisions to be made as closely as possible to delivery to the customer.

- Our structure ensures people identify with their customer and with the product they produce.

DECISION-MAKING AND INFORMATION SYSTEM

- Individuals and groups know which outcomes they are responsible for and understand how the work they do contributes to the mission and outcomes.

- Individuals most affected by a decision will be meaningfully involved in making that decision.

PEOPLE SYSTEM

- The selection system is based on having people demonstrate their competency in technical, social, and business skills and their potential for leadership.

- All our people receive sufficient training to do their jobs and keep their skills and knowledge current throughout their careers.

- All our people have the opportunity to acquire multiple skills through education, training, and/or lateral movement; all employees are encouraged to use these opportunities.

REWARD SYSTEM

- Individuals and teams are rewarded for their contributions to the achievement of team and organizational goals.

- Rewards reinforce desired behaviors instead of punishing undesired ones.

DESIGN CHOICES

- Design choices are reviewed periodically.

- Renewal is everybody's responsibility.

- Our business systems, processes, and structures support innovation and continuous improvement.

OSD TOOL SETS

We use three tool sets to carrying out a design effort: 1) environmental scan, 2) process analysis, and 3) culture analysis. Using these tools yields information about how current design choices align and what future choices should be designed to accomplish (e.g., outstanding performance, building a team of leaders).

Make note: Every tool does not have to be used in order to achieve a successful redesign effort. However, the more information that is gathered through the use of these tools, the more likely it will be that the team will make the best possible design choices.

Successful design projects gather data about the market and the economic environment first, before they turn to process analysis. But team design doesn't stop with a close look at your team processes—it moves on to understand social and cultural aspects as well.

Let's look at each one of these tool sets in more detail, recognizing that the limitations of this book do not allow us to go over each tool in full detail.

ENVIRONMENTAL SCAN

Designing for success begins with environmental scanning, which is the first tool set. The idea is to verify or discover what your customers and other stakeholders value most. This series of tools will help you understand these requirements better.

Teams are "open systems"—they exist in an environment that influences them. Political realities, the media, and global economic swings are examples of environmental factors that impact the needs of customers and your team's approaches to serving them. Environmental scanning is a review of the groups outside your team that most affect the team. It is a study of the specific requirements of those groups, and an inquiry into how those requirements might be changed. The knowledge gathered during environmental scanning helps you make better design choices.

A good way to begin environmental scanning is to identify the important groups or elements in your environment. As stated previously, you probably have five general categories of groups in your environment: customers, stakeholders, influencers, competitors, and best-in-class organizations.

Another step in your environmental scan is to determine what you already know about these groups, what you don't know that you need to know, and how you will get the information you need. Customer and stakeholder interviews or surveys are a good way to flesh out your knowledge and gather what you need to know. These efforts capture the "voice of the customer."

A good example of the value of this method occurred with a series of claims processing teams we worked with. Prior to scanning the environment, senior leaders believed that in order to satisfy customers, they needed to process claims within a certain number of days (with the number of days varying, depending on what the senior leadership team in power at the time believed was appropriate).

However, when they actually scanned their customers, they were shocked to find out they didn't really care what the timeliness goal was. The important thing to customers was to be told in advance how long it would take for a claim to be processed and then to live up to the expected completion date. Moreover, if the claim was going to take longer than expected, customers wanted to be so advised.

This was a very different way of looking at expectations, and one the team's leaders never would have been aware of had they not conducted an environmental scan.

A final step in scanning the environment is to document your findings and draw conclusions. Make sure you capture design choice ideas as they arise and also as you complete your environmental scanning efforts.

The conclusions you reach about the requirements of your external environment will have an impact on other design choices in your team. That is why you should look back on your environmental scan data. Consider the impact on the business and the implications for design. Then use the OSD Model for Teams to organize your thinking about design choices.

PROCESS ANALYSIS

Once customer and stakeholder requirements are understood, we turn our attention inward, to your team's processes. This analysis is also called *process management* or *technical analysis*. It draws upon the principles that teams are composed of processes, and not all processes are created equal.

This is the time to carefully analyze your processes and understand how well they are working. You need to prioritize them; to recognize the bottlenecks in the processes that are slowing you down; to identify any deviations from your standard procedures; to figure out the relationship between upstream mistakes and how they cascade downstream; to determine who owns each process; and to examine how important decisions are made.

There are seven process analysis tools: 1) process mapping, 2) categorization of work, 3) value analysis, 4) constraint analysis, 5) variance analysis, 6) process management, and 7) key decision analysis. A full description of all the available tools for process analysis is not possible, given the many tools that exist and the broad scope of this book. However, these seven methods for analyzing your processes are briefly described here, followed by some examples of the actual tools available.

- *Process mapping* is a tool that helps you visualize the flow of work in an organization and identify the points within a process where value is created. Process maps are an essential tool for grasping and communicating your organization's work.

- *Categorization of work* is a process for distilling your work into one of several categories—competitive work, competitive enabling work, essential work, compliance work, and nonessential work—in order to determine the work's priority.

- *Value analysis* is where you identify which tasks are value-added and which are not, and then reduce or eliminate non-value-added tasks.

- *Constraint analysis* is a tool that helps you identify the point(s) in the process most responsible for slowing it down and limiting the team from achieving higher performance.

- *Variance analysis* is a series of tools for finding and eliminating mistakes and defects.

- *Process management* begins as process analysis wraps up. Here is where the team considers who will own each business process. After all, every process should have an owner.

- *Key decision analysis* is where the team looks at the decisions associated with any given process. For example, a key decision chart is often used to pinpoint the key decisions in a business process and clarify which individuals and groups have responsibility for those decisions. This helps the team analyze knowledge work for a given business process. Revealing and resolving ambiguities in decision-making activities ultimately results in clear roles and responsibilities.

Figure 2-3 is an example of how work is categorized.

Figure 2-4 is an example of a constraint analysis tool, used for identifying bottlenecks in a process.

As you can see, these are just a few examples of a holistic and comprehensive approach toward analyzing your core processes. Using these methods and tools will provide the team with an unprecedented degree

FIGURE 2-3. Categorization of work.

Categorization of Work Decision Tree

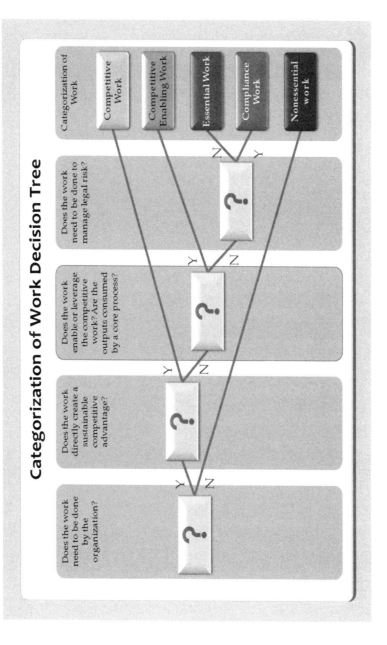

Does the work need to be done by the organization?

Does the work directly create a sustainable competitive advantage?

Does the work enable or leverage the competitive work? Are the outputs consumed by a core process?

Does the work need to be done to manage legal risk?

Categorization of Work

Competitive Work

Competitive Enabling Work

Essential Work

Compliance Work

Nonessential work

FIGURE 2-4. Constraint analysis.

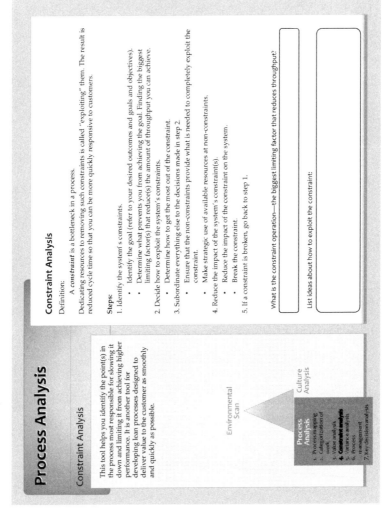

Process Analysis

Constraint Analysis

This tool helps you identify the point(s) in the process most responsible for slowing it down and limiting it from achieving higher performance. It is another tool for developing lean processes designed to deliver value to the customer as smoothly and quickly as possible.

Environmental
Scan

Culture
Analysis

**Process
Analysis**
1. Process mapping
2. Categorization of
 work
3. Value analysis
4. **Constraint analysis**
5. Variance analysis
6. Process
 management
7. Key decision analysis

Constraint Analysis

Definition:

A *constraint* is a bottleneck in a process.

Dedicating resources to removing such constraints is called "exploiting" them. The result is reduced cycle time so that you can be more quickly responsive to customers.

Steps:

1. Identify the system's constraints.
 - Identify the goal (refer to your desired outcomes and goals and objectives).
 - Determine what prevents you from achieving the goal. Finding the biggest limiting factor(s) that reduce(s) the amount of throughput you can achieve.
2. Decide how to exploit the system's constraints.
 - Determine how to get the most out of the constraint.
3. Subordinate everything else to the decisions made in step 2.
 - Ensure that the non-constraints provide what is needed to completely exploit the constraint.
 - Make strategic use of available resources at non-constraints.
4. Reduce the impact of the system's constraint(s).
 - Reduce the impact of the constraint on the system.
 - Break the constraint.
5. If a constraint is broken, go back to step 1.

What is the constraint operation—the biggest limiting factor that reduces throughput?

List ideas about how to exploit the constraint:

of information and understanding of its core work that will enable the team to refine its processes (to the maximum extent possible) and ensure that it is working in an effective and efficient manner.

Once some or all of the seven process analysis tools have been completed, as appropriate, the next step is to gather together any and all ideas that have been generated about possible changes to the organizational design. The conclusions you reach through process management will have an impact on your business and implications for your structure and other design choices in your team.

CULTURE ANALYSIS

The culture analysis tool set helps you study knowledge, networks, and culture in your team. Using information from process analysis about your distinctive processes, you can seek to understand what knowledge is distinctive and determine how well that knowledge is being converted into customer value. Culture analysis will also look at how well your team renews its knowledge base. In other words, you will study your learning capability.

You will also study the networks surrounding critical roles in the team. Much knowledge, by its very nature, cannot be shared outside the context of active, trusting, cooperative relationships—the right people talking to the right people about the right things at the right time.

The culture analysis tool kit contains the following assessments:

- *Interaction network analysis* is a means of assessing the communication patterns and networks within a team. It helps diagnose where collaboration has collapsed or cliques have been cultivated, where talent and expertise could be better leveraged, where decisions are bottlenecked, or where opportunities for leadership and/or innovation are being lost.

- *Individual needs assessment* is designed to determine the extent to which the needs of each individual in a team are met. The idea here is to rank the team members' overall satisfaction with the way their needs are being met and then address these findings when making future design choices.

- *Voice of the team assessment* determines how well the members of a team display the behaviors, feelings, and attributes needed to drive the organization to its desired outcomes. This assessment is very different from asking team members how satisfied they are. It is focused on understanding specific culture attributes and design choices in a team and their relationship to high performance. One organization that we worked with was able to identify five specific items that contributed to a 20 percent difference between high-performing and average-performing teams. Organizational leaders then were able to work with teams throughout their company by zeroing in on these five items that were differentiating factors of high performance.

- *Knowledge assessment* links design choices about process changes, new structures, and other improvements with the corresponding development of beliefs, skills, and information.

- *Skills matrix,* the final culture analysis tool, helps outline the skills and skill levels needed by a team. A completed skills matrix is a useful template for training and selection initiatives.

Now let's give examples of several of these tools.

The interaction network analysis seeks to map networks in order to make visible the connections where information sharing, decision making, and innovation either thrive or falter. Here are the steps for completing such an analysis, using the template provided in Figure 2-5:

1. Identify critical roles in the team.

2. Identify the direction of the interaction with an arrow between roles. (Who initiated the interaction?)

3. Identify the frequency of the interaction by writing it on the arrow (1 = too little, 2 = just right, 3 = too much).

4. Identify the content of the interaction by writing it on the line between the two roles.

5. Identify the effectiveness of the interaction with an H for high satisfaction, M for medium, and L for low. (Did the interaction get results?)

6. List suggestions for improvement.

With respect to individual needs, people only bring so much energy to work. If individual needs are met, people will most likely channel their energy in a positive direction. But if their individual needs are not met, people tend to devote energy to counterproductive purposes in the team. Figure 2-6 is an example of an individual needs assessment that can be conducted in five steps.

FIGURE 2-5. Interaction network analysis.

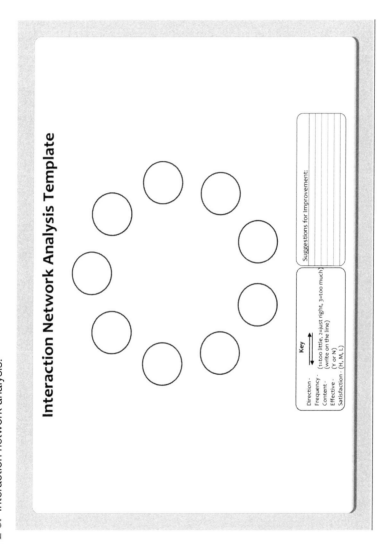

FIGURE 2-6. Individual needs assessment.

| Step 1 | *Write down* your answer to the following question: I am most energized in my work when: |

_____

_____

Now think of any role in life that you enjoy or have enjoyed in the past. Some examples of roles include coach, parent, choir member, fisherman, and bowling team member. Record your answer to the following question:
I am most energized in this role in life when:

_____

_____

| Step 2 | *Share* your answers with your team. Look for individual needs that your team has in common, and then list them. |

| Step 3 | *Rank* the needs your team has listed using a multi-voting technique of your choosing. One way might be to give everyone five votes. Each person distributes his or her votes in any way desired—for example, five votes to the need the person feels is most important, or three votes to one need and two to another, or one vote to each of five needs. Then, when everyone is finished voting, total the votes for each need. The need with the most votes is ranked first, the need with the second most votes is ranked second, and so on. |

| Step 4 | As a group, determine your overall level of satisfaction (H = High, M = Medium, or L = Low) for each need. |

| Step 5 | *Discuss* design choices that lowered the level of satisfaction ratings, and suggest design choices that might improve the ratings in the future. |

Note that the knowledge assessment, voice of the team assessment, and the skills matrix will be discussed in greater detail in Chapter 5 (Developing and Managing Knowledge Is Key to Team Performance).

PUTTING IT ALL TOGETHER

Using the three team design analysis tools—environmental scan, process analysis, and culture analysis—we have shown so far what data are important, how to gather them, and how to consider their implications for design. We have also referred to the OSD Model for Teams to help us organize our thinking.

Now the real design work begins. If you were following the entire process as described so far, you would have been mostly *analyzing*—that is, analyzing the environment, the technical system, and the social system. It would now be time to stop analyzing and engage in a much more creative activity.

To start, you would review the data you have gathered, but then free your mind by asking:

- *What if* we were to completely rub out all the existing procedures, practices, rules, workflows, block diagrams, and task listings?

- *What if* we were to completely demolish the way the work is done?

- *What if* we could do the work any way we wanted?

- *What if* we were to start with a completely blank sheet of paper?

- *How* can we build a team of leaders?

Designing a team that meets the needs of the environment, the technical system, and the social system is called *joint optimization*. When going through this process, a team must also consider the *alignment* of its choices. One of the most important yet challenging activities in design is to ensure that all the design elements are in alignment and work in harmony to drive the culture and desired outcomes.

A good example of a lack of alignment occurred when Paul was engaged to help an energy company that had embraced teams. The company had already invested a lot of money to take its teams offsite and put them through a series of team-building activities, such as ropes courses and climbing walls and trust falls and walks. The company did a survey of the workforce and found that teamwork was rated lower than it had been before.

Paul learned that in the April/May time frame, the team managers went offsite and rated and ranked each person on the team using a zero-sum scale and then told the employees what their rating was. Employees were outraged as they suddenly felt they were competing with one another as opposed to working together as a team. All the time, energy, and money that had been devoted to building a sense of teamwork had been lost.

In this case, one design element had a major adverse impact simply because the reward system only rewarded individual performance and discouraged teamwork.

In a somewhat similar situation, Stew was asked to work with a series of teams at another organization. When he first walked around the work environment, he was struck by the fact that most of the employees were situated behind five-foot-tall partitions.

The net affect of this design was that employees seated in their cubicle could only see the person sitting directly across from them and no one else. They could not see any other person unless they or someone else happened to be walking around. It resulted in the employees becoming inwardly focused and less likely to work together as a team.

Obviously, this crucial design element was out of alignment relative to many of the other choices that were in place to encourage teamwork (e.g., group rewards, frequent team meetings), and it made the objective of having a team environment much more challenging to achieve.

Once you have drawn up a creative set of final design choice recommendations, test them for joint optimization. Ask yourself: How can all the needs that were made apparent by the three analyses be met? Then check for alignment. Do all your recommended choices drive the outcomes you want? Will they ultimately enable you to reach Stage Five and build a team of leaders?

Be sure to compare your design choice recommendations with the design guidelines we outlined previously in this chapter. Consider whether all the recommendations fall within the boundaries of the guidelines.

A good example of a successful redesign effort occurred at a large segment of a company that reinvented itself by relocating its office and redesigning its management structure with a focus on teamwork. The company headed for a greenfield site with an open mind about structure and design. The idea was to start anew and develop an organization with a strong and human-focused culture.

The move to a new location was the first of two significant changes. The second occurred a year later, when the company hired an organizational systems design (OSD) consulting firm to ensure that all the sociotechnical parts were properly aligned.

Although the company had redesigned its management structure, it had basically retained the same workflow and design—as a result, the strain of having a new technical system and an outdated social system resulted in a misalignment.

With the help of OSD consultant Paul Gustavson, the company began to ask such questions as: Where do we want to go in the future? What do we want to be? How is work being done now?

From there, the company created a series of design teams to analyze their systems, workflow, and processes, using many of the OSD tools described in this chapter. For example, after determining the state changes in each workflow, the design teams sought to identify the "variances" associated with each step. After determining the costs of these variances, they built variance control mechanisms into the system.

Given the opportunity to make significant changes in their processes and methods, the excitement and energy level among the design team members increased as they recognized that their ideas and suggested changes were now valued. Eventually, model customer-focused teams were set up throughout the organization using the principles described in this book. Meanwhile, managers began to assume the roles of "facilitator" and "consultant" and also began to focus more on cross-functional issues and the external environment.

Within the larger organization, this component became known as a model of an innovative and participative work culture. In fact, it became common to see executives and potential customers from all over the country come to visit and learn about this division's technical, organizational, and cultural practices.

Among the many successes, one team saw its cost per unit of work decline by roughly 75 percent. This improvement was accomplished by an increase of individual productivity by almost 100 percent, a reduction in the number of managers and staff positions, and the teams' tight control of costly variances.[1]

Figure 2-7 illustrates how the joint optimization process works. It shows that during joint optimization, you should look at all the systems and design choices holistically in order to ensure they fit together in the best possible design.

FIGURE 2-7. Joint optimization of a team design.

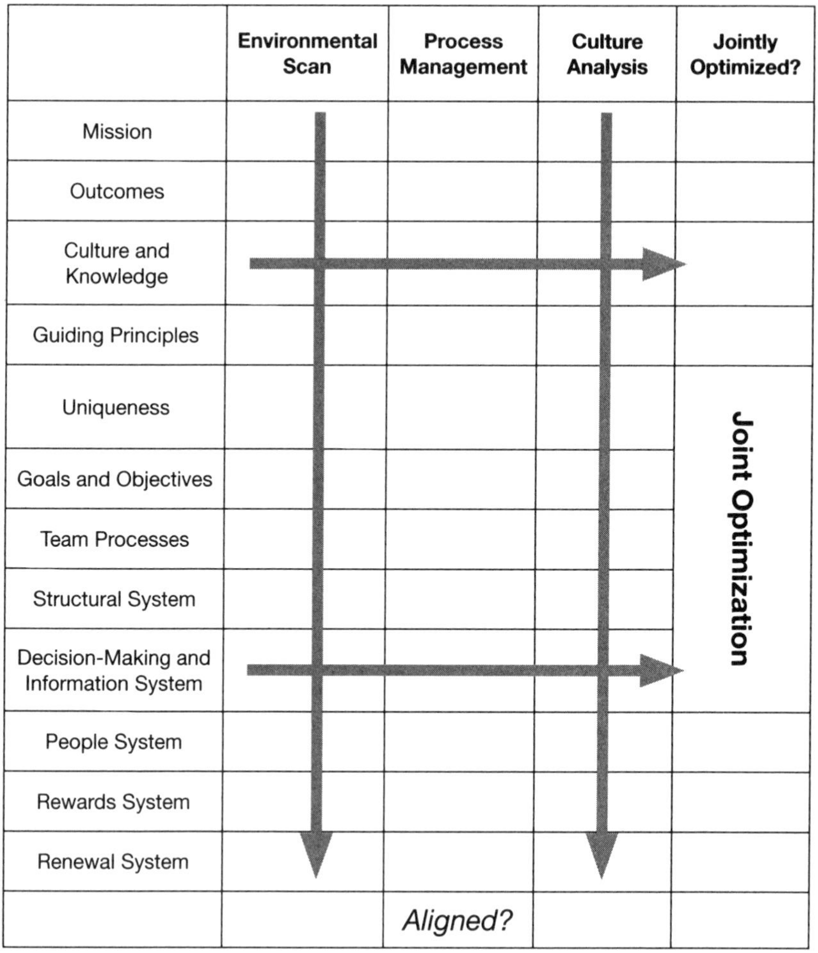

	Environmental Scan	Process Management	Culture Analysis	Jointly Optimized?
Mission				
Outcomes				
Culture and Knowledge				
Guiding Principles				
Uniqueness				
Goals and Objectives				
Team Processes				
Structural System				
Decision-Making and Information System				
People System				
Rewards System				
Renewal System				
		Aligned?		

TRANSITION PLANNING

Once your analysis work is complete and the design has been finalized, you need to turn your attention to implementing the design. Good implementation naturally begins with careful transition planning.

You will need to consider how to move from the old team practices to new ones. What steps must be taken to develop the proposed design changes?

Careful transition planning is crucial because in the middle of any change effort, people are likely to long for "the way it used to be"—even though they might not have liked the old way at the time. Always ask the question, "How will we manage this sentiment?"

To make things happen as smoothly as possible, we actually recommend a series of plans, or five types of transition plans:

1. A Management Plan to define who will pay attention to day-to-day business, and who will be at least temporarily reassigned to lead, plan, and manage the change

2. An Action Plan to identify transition activities, and then to sequence, time, and assign responsibility for the implementation of the design choices

3. A Stakeholder Commitment Plan to determine who needs to be committed to the design, where those people are now, and where they need to be

4. An Evaluation Plan to ensure that the design is doing what was intended and to watch that design drift doesn't set in

5. A Stabilization Plan to discourage the natural tendency to revert to the old organization

CHALLENGES, TENSIONS, AND KEY FACTORS DURING IMPLEMENTATION

The biggest challenge in doing a redesign effort is the amount of time and energy that is involved in going through the process. There is no doubt that this could be a turnoff for some people, especially those who are not convinced that the effort is needed or worthwhile. The best way to deal with the naysayers is to ask them if their team is performing up to its capability and if they are experiencing the challenges that we outlined in Chapter 1. If they agree there is an opportunity to improve, educate them about the value of a team redesign.

Once a decision is made to move forward, there are several ways to reduce the overall burden. First of all, as stated previously, you do not have to use every one of the OSD redesign tools. If you are confident that some of the information needed for your analyses is already available, then don't use the tool designed to gather that information. Just make sure that you have enough information for the final joint optimization decisions.

Second, the transition planning methodology is intended to address many of the tensions that naturally exist when you are trying to redesign the team while trying to keep up with the workload. Simply ensure you have the right players on the transition planning team so that your five plans are in line and carefully monitored.

Finally, make it clear to the players that once the team decides to move forward, participation is not optional—they are either in or out. There is no other choice. If someone wants to opt out, help transition that person to another spot either inside or, preferably, outside the overall organization. For everyone else, get them involved in the redesign effort in some way or another. In this way, it will increase their buy-in and begin their conversion from followers to leaders.

HOW REDESIGNING YOUR SYSTEMS WILL HELP BUILD LEADERS

If you look again at the OSD Model for Teams, you will clearly see that a team's knowledge and culture are driven by its design choices and desired outcomes. Simply put, for a team to 1) have a culture where all its members are energetic, empowered, and knowledgeable leaders and 2) produce outstanding results, it must make the right design choices based on careful review and analysis. Moreover, all these choices must be properly aligned to drive the right behaviors, feelings, and attributes of the team's members.

In other words, to produce a team of leaders, a team must be perfectly designed to get that result.

CHAPTER

Teams Have Processes, Too

***Key principle:** All your processes must support the goal of making everyone a leader.*

TEAMS ARE GENERALLY PART of a larger organization and at least one of its processes (e.g., product development, demand creation, supply chain); by the same token, teams have their own processes, which are essential to carrying out the team's purpose and objectives. These processes include performing the core work of the team, managing team performance, selecting and on-boarding new members, building capability of the team and its members, and managing the disengagement or deselecting of team members.

This chapter will help you think about how to identify your team's processes. It will also walk you through the aforementioned processes and offer examples of how to think about and design your own processes.

PERFORMING THE CORE WORK

Every team has its core work to perform. However, for everyone to ultimately become a leader, the team as a whole needs to understand how that work actually flows so that it can make sure that work is being performed as effectively and efficiently as possible.

An excellent way to examine how core work is performed is through the process analysis process, which we introduced in the last chapter. The best way to get started is through process mapping, which is a tool that helps you visualize the flow of work and identify the points within a process where value is created. It is an essential tool for grasping and communicating your team's work. Let's look at this issue in a bit more depth.

Subsets of activities where value is created in distinct and measurable ways are called state changes. A state change is a collection of work activities where the characteristics of the product or service are essentially changed or converted. For example, an information request may be changed to an accepted request that may then be changed to an answer. State changes are the building blocks by which an organization/team creates a product or service that is valuable to its buyers.

A process is usually made up of several state changes, as the example in Figure 3-1 illustrates.

A more detailed illustration of the state changes for a sample specialty bakery is shown in Figure 3-2.

By looking at your work in this manner, it will help your team map and define the strategic impact of your processes and activities. It will also help you identify waste and variability and bottlenecks in your processes.

FIGURE 3-1. State changes (simple).

FIGURE 3-2. Stage changes (complex).

State Change Process Map: Specialty Bakery

Baking

Invoicing

Mixing

Delivering

Procurement

Packaging

Cash Application

Ordering

Decorating

Payment

From there, your team can then turn to some or all of the six remaining process analysis tools mentioned in the previous chapter (e.g., categorization of work, value analysis, constraint analysis, among others). They will provide you with that much more detail for an unprecedented degree of information and understanding of your core work; your team will then be able to analyze and prioritize your processes to the maximum extent possible.

For example, after conducting a series of reviews and analyses, your team may decide that one (or more) of its processes is nonessential; the team can then either eliminate the process or farm it out. Or your team may decide that while a process is essential, it should be revised in order to make it more effective and efficient.

Let's take a look at an organization whose teams found a better way to approach an issue. This organization consistently did from $2 billion to $3 billion of business per year and decided that it needed to reduce waste and eliminate non-value-added activities.

The approach taken was a refreshing one. Rather than focus on simply cutting costs, the organization emphasized reducing costs in order to *grow* the business rather than shrink it. As a result, the employees did not see this decision as another management ploy to reduce the workforce and place their jobs in jeopardy. Instead, they viewed it as a positive approach that could help both them and the company, which was a concept everyone could rally around.

Initially, cost-reduction goals were set for each vice president, which produced some modest savings but relatively little buy-in. However, the following year, the company developed teams of employees to look at the issue of waste in much more depth. The company discovered that when the employees started working together as teams, something magical began to happen because people are better at reducing waste when they work together. They met with each other, started exchanging ideas, shared best practices, and also determined the paths that were not worth following.

As they moved forward, they decided to focus on reviewing their business processes. They looked at each process, categorized the work accordingly and, where appropriate, made modifications using the principle that they had to either do different things or do things differently. Throughout their reviews, they found that the best way to save money was during those points in the process when something was handed off.

During a five-year period, the teams saved this company roughly half a billion dollars, with an initial savings of $100 million to $150 million for the first couple of years. Not only that, the systemic changes identified during these reviews provided them with a distinct competitive advantage.

Another private sector company had a contracts processing team, with fifty people involved in some aspect of processing contracts. The problem was that there were so many different people involved in the process with multiple handoffs (e.g., someone received the contract, another took it out of a bundle, a person reviewed the information, a different one entered information into the computer system, someone else checked the information, still another scanned it, etc.) that no one owned the process.

The company decided to form a new team, called Team Two, which was composed of ten employees. All these team members were cross-trained on how to perform virtually every task, and they wound up doing everything from start to finish (except for the digital scanning, which remained a separate part of the process for technical reasons).

The net result was that production increased dramatically and fewer people were needed to manage the entire process. Moreover, the process became more efficient and it took far less time to process the contracts. For example, during one particular week, it cost Team One $4.98 to process a unit, while it cost Team Two only $1.56 per unit. This 3:1 unit cost disparity stayed relatively consistent, which was especially significant since the organization processed about 172,000 units. As you would expect, the company eventually decided to use the Team Two concept to process all its contracts work.

Looking at the core work will also result in a change in your team's thinking. Instead of seeing their jobs as pushing a button, team members will see themselves as part of a state change or conversion process. For example, they might see themselves as taking calls and converting them to solutions, as opposed to thinking they are simply a call-taking center.

It works the same way as energy, which is neither created nor destroyed; it just changes its state. So does water, which changes to ice, to steam, and back to water. Rather than being activity driven, we begin to think of the team and its individual processes as changing the states of an input until it becomes a final output … and that is a huge change in thinking.

MANAGING PERFORMANCE

Every team must manage its own performance. That is no great revelation. However, to self-manage properly, your team must manage both its own performance and the individual performance of its members in a holistic and comprehensive manner. More important, it must use an integrated performance management system that works in conjunction with the other systems described previously in this chapter.

Let's talk about performance management at both the team and individual levels.

PERFORMANCE AT THE TEAM LEVEL

First and foremost, your team needs to have goals and objectives that are expressed as metrics. (Sample metrics were provided in Chapter 2.) The metrics must then be clearly aligned with what the overall organization is trying to accomplish.

These metrics should be shared with every team member so that they will know what to strive for. Members should also receive a clear explanation as to what the metrics mean, where they come from, and how they are tracked, so they will know how they can best achieve them.

Of course, team members must receive the appropriate tools and training to help them achieve their goals. Otherwise, they will merely be spinning their wheels. Much more information on this subject can be found in Chapter 5, Developing and Managing Knowledge Is Key to Team Performance.

The metrics themselves, as well as team performance relative to them, should be strategically posted throughout the team work area so that all team members know exactly what is expected of them and how they are doing. Such an approach will make it clear to everyone that performance is important and will ensure there are no secrets or surprises regarding how the team is doing. Posting performance information (at both the team and the individual levels) is part of a broader performance improvement strategy known as Visual Management, which we will discuss extensively in Chapter 6.

The team should meet on a periodic basis (daily, weekly, or monthly) as appropriate. The frequency of these meetings should be based on a variety of factors: the availability of the data, how often things change, and the current level of performance, for example (although these meetings, for the most part, should be relatively brief). Preferably, the meetings should take place in an area that contains the posted information so that everyone can speak from fact rather than merely express an opinion.

During these meetings, the team should review areas where improvement is needed, such as resources, expectations, attendance, equipment failure, and training needs. For example, one team we worked with had a problem with accountability. Its job was to rehabilitate certain disadvantaged clients, which means the team was supposed to help these people find jobs. However, since one person evaluated customers' needs, another placed them in training, and a third tried to find them a job, no one owned the process. As a result, whenever problems developed, these different individuals would point the finger at someone else on the team, claiming that it was not their fault.

Once team members came to grips with the problem, they decided to include the number of clients that were rehabilitated in *everyone's* standard—even though they all only owned a part of the process. This prompted all the team members to work together, find solutions, and stop passing the buck. Communication improved significantly, and the number of clients that were rehabilitated skyrocketed.

Periodically, your team should also look at how each team member is contributing to the overall team performance. A team is only as strong as its weakest link, after all, and the more team members work together to lift everyone's performance, the better.

We therefore recommend that teams post every member's performance on a spreadsheet in the same area where they post the team's performance. We suggest that this information be posted anonymously (i.e., with a letter representing each team member in order to protect people's privacy). However, you can expect that people will talk to one another about these statistics, and there will be peer pressure to both rise to the top and lift the performance of the employees at the bottom of the spreadsheet.

Figure 3-3 is an example of how to post information on team member performance. Note that the spreadsheet not only includes performance information; it also includes information about each person's attendance. This is clearly a different way of thinking about performance since many employees and unions tend to argue that attendance is separate and distinct from performance. However, think about it this way: Even if the employee is producing a lot of work on average, if he or she is rarely at work, is that *really* contributing to your *team's* success? That is the type of thought process that we want every team member/future leader to have.

During regularly scheduled meetings, your team should always be on the lookout for variations in processes. You want your team members

FIGURE 3-3. Sample posting of employee performance.

Employee	Output	Accuracy	Timeliness	Hrs Absent
A	4.6 (97)	86%	93%	8
B	4.1 (83)	98%	90%	14
C	4.1 (90)	88%	80%	0
D	3.8 (72)	83%	100%	24
E	3.5 (60)	85%	90%	40
F	3.1 (68)	90%	88%	0

Standard	3.5	90%	90%	N/A
Team Average	4.0	87%	90%	14

As you can see, this posting contains excellent information for the team to have. Note the impact of employee absence on output, particularly as it applies to Employee E.

focusing on their systems/processes, which are usually the root cause of significant problems, as opposed to merely looking for someone to blame. If not, downstream they will eventually find out the hard way where their process problems lie.

MANAGING INDIVIDUAL PERFORMANCE

To a large extent, the approach the team takes with individual performance management should be the same one it uses for group performance. First of all, each employee should know what is expected of him. Within this context, individual performance standards should be closely aligned with your team's goals and objectives. If they are not, the employees will focus on areas that are not important, which will lead to a diffusion of the team's energy.

Wherever possible, each employee's performance plan should contain a mix of measures covering such areas as output or productivity, quality, timeliness, customer satisfaction, employee development, organizational support, and teamwork. There should also be a measure that both drives and reflects the degree to which each employee is assuming leadership within the team.

The employee should receive periodic feedback as to how she is doing relative to the performance standards, preferably on a monthly or quarterly basis. The feedback should be both oral and in writing as appropriate, via some form of a report card. Figure 3-4 is an example of such a report card.

FIGURE 3-4. Sample employee report card.

Month	Output	Accuracy	Timeliness	Leave Taken (Hrs)
Oct	3.8 (84)	88%	91%	0
Nov	4.0 (84)	90%	100%	8
Dec	4.2 (87)	85%	88%	11
Jan	3.9 (74)	100%	90%	24
Feb	4.4 (97)	90%	100%	0
Mar	3.9 (85)	92%	90%	8

Standard	3.5	90%	90%	N/A
Your Average	4.0 (85)	93%	94%	8.3
Team Average	3.8 (83)	91%	91%	6.1

Using a report card provides the employee with periodic, written feedback so that there are no surprises and no secrets. Note that under Output, the overall number of widgets per month is also provided, in addition to the average, because that gives a more complete picture of the employee's contribution.

*Information regarding less definable measures, such as employee development, organizational support, etc., should be added to the spreadsheet in narrative form.

Regarding the feedback, the immediate supervisor should initially provide it, although as your team moves through the five stages of team development, this role should gravitate to the team. Feedback should be honest and forthright and let the employee know exactly how she is doing and what she needs to do to improve. The employee should also be given the opportunity to express her opinion as to how things are going and articulate any areas where she believes help is needed.

Should the employee have an individual development plan (IDP), the performance feedback session would be a good time to go over this plan as well. Ensuring that employees' training needs are met is in everybody's best interest, so incorporating this discussion within the context of a performance management feedback session makes sense. However, it should be consistent with the principles we describe in Chapter 5 (Developing and Managing Knowledge Is Key to Team Performance).

The key to employee performance management, regardless of your team's current stage, is ensuring there are reliable consequences for every level of performance. That is, excellent employees should be recognized and rewarded commensurate with their contribution, average employees should retain their jobs and receive all the appropriate benefits, and action should be taken to deal with poor performers.

In other words, employees should be able to see an action coming, whether it is good, neutral, or bad. It should almost never be a surprise. Employees will then conclude that the system works as intended, will consistently follow the rules and processes, and will strive to achieve the team's goals and objectives. Moreover, they will go the extra mile because they will see that their coworkers cannot merely coast and receive the same pay and rating as them.

On the other hand, if they believe management (or eventually the team) goes after people it doesn't like, regardless of their performance, and protects favorites, even if they are poor performers, then employees will conclude that the system is meaningless and it is every man for himself. If this happens, focus and trust will dissipate and your team will be in real trouble.

Rewards and recognition go hand in hand with sound performance management. Unfortunately, more often than not, rewards and recognition programs wind up being *disincentive* awards programs because they reward the wrong things and send the wrong message.

There are several keys to an effective program:

- The rewards program must be aligned and consistent with your team's goals.

- As your team grows, the team members should be involved in developing and/or reviewing the rewards targets.

- These targets should be published in advance, with team members receiving frequent feedback as to how the team and they are doing relative to these targets.

- Targets/rewards should be available at both the group and individual levels in order to encourage people to work together and also do their best.

- The rewards must be reliably distributed based solely on performance/behavior and not on personality or "who you know."

Of course, recognition is also an important part of any incentive awards program. Simply saying "thank you" to a contributing team member goes a long way toward reinforcing the right performance and retaining team members. Selecting a team member of the month, having a quarterly awards breakfast/luncheon for the team, giving out and posting "thank you" cards, or even developing a video highlighting the team's and/or an employee's success are all simple but effective ways of recognizing success.

An innovative and inexpensive program that proved very effective was one in which each team member was given ten awards certificates to distribute to coworkers as appropriate. The certificates listed the team's core values. Anytime a team member did something that reinforced these values, another team member could give that certificate to his teammate in recognition. Each time someone received a signed certificate, he was to place it in a locked box. At the end of each quarter, several certificates would be selected from that box at random, with each person named on the certificate receiving two tickets to a local restaurant.

SELECTING AND ON-BOARDING NEW MEMBERS

High-performing teams participate in the selection of their members. If that's the practice of your team, then your team will have much more at stake in its own success and exhibit a different level of ownership and commitment. A high level of ownership and commitment comes from the processes, and high-performing teams have better processes and do a better job of selecting and on-boarding their new members.

Before we go forward, it is important to consider the following question: When does the selection process end? During the selection process? When an offer is made? The first day the employee reports for work? When the employee is contributing? The answer is that the selection process ends when the individual is a net giver rather than a net receiver equal to her cost. Once an employee reaches this point, she then moves on to the "building capability" process. (This topic is discussed further in a subsequent section of this chapter.)

Let's now look at the selection and on-boarding processes in greater detail.

SELECTION PROCESS

Selecting the right person is one of the most important decisions your team can make. After all, the process of hiring is time-consuming and fraught with risk (e.g., you can hire the wrong person or someone who isn't selected may file a complaint). Once a person is hired, though, your team will invest an enormous amount of time and energy in developing the employee. If she proves to be a bad fit, more time will then be spent trying to turn her around and, if necessary, firing her, in which case the process starts all over again.

That is why having a set of guiding principles for the selection process is so important. These principles help ensure that the selection process is fair and comprehensive and results in the best candidate being chosen. In applying these principles, it is essential that everyone involved in the process understands and agrees to a set of guiding principles.

We've identified the following guiding principles as best practices when selecting new team members:

- We will make our hiring decisions based on developed criteria, which will include the goal of only selecting someone who has the potential to be a leader within the team.

- We will not compromise the selection criteria or process; it is the cornerstone of our performance and development process.

- Self-selection at each step is the key to the selection process. We will provide enough information for candidates to choose for themselves whether this position is for them.

- The best predictor of future behavior is past behavior, where past behavior replicates what behavior is being asked for in the future.

- Where there is no past experience, we will create opportunities to demonstrate future performance (e.g., scenarios, simulations, role-plays, presentations, in-basket exercises).

- We will create opportunities for all critical elements of the selection criteria to be demonstrated in the selection process.

- The selection methodology will ensure that participants are able to demonstrate the capabilities they have to offer.

- Our selection process is the cornerstone to hiring the best people for the job and thus is key to the success of our business.

- Given a choice between two candidates, we will select the one that requires the least development (best fit).

- The output of the selection process is the input into an ongoing development process.

- After the selection is made, we will gather feedback from those individuals selected to ensure that the process works as designed.

Naturally, you can tweak these principles and customize them for your team. The key is that they be consistent with your values, systems, and processes and result in the selection of the right people for your team.

ON-BOARDING

This is your opportunity to have your new hires get off to a good start. It is your only chance to shape the new employees' first impression of your team and the organization, so you want to do everything you can to leverage each person's energy and enthusiasm. If you don't, you may quickly find that your new employees become cynical because of the way they are treated and the wrong message(s) they get.

It is always a shame to see new employees report for orientation in a dark and depressing room. Moreover, they may then have a series of bland and uninspired speakers address them who unintentionally (or perhaps intentionally) send a message that they really don't want to be attending the session. Imagine how that makes the newcomers feel on their first day of work. Is it any wonder that so many people get turned off so quickly?

Fortunately, there are a number of tried-and-true strategies that have been proven to work when on-boarding new employees. Let's list some of these strategies:

- Provide at least a two- to four-hour orientation session to the new team members. Hold the session in a bright and vibrant area that makes it clear the employees are valued.

- Bring in a series of knowledgeable and enthusiastic speakers, including the team leader, who can address issues of importance to the attendees and answer their questions.

- Address these topics, among others, in this session:

  – The history of the organization/team

  – Its mission, vision, and core values

  – Critical issues the organization/team faces

  – Expectations

  – Human resources management issues (pay, promotions, awards, benefits)

  – Union issues, if any

  – Questions and answers

- Use the orientation session to conduct individual skill assessments as well. They will allow management and/or the team to identify strengths and weaknesses of the new employees and determine where gaps exist within the team.

- Assign a mentor to each new hire to work directly with the employee from day one. Moreover, these mentors should continue to work with your new hires on a regular basis in order to get them off on the right foot and assist them in navigating their way through the system.

BUILDING CAPABILITY OF THE TEAM AND ITS MEMBERS

This is a critical part of the overall process; after all, your team will never achieve its potential if its members are not capable of performing at a high level. Because we are going to discuss this issue in great detail in Chapter 5, Developing and Managing Knowledge Is Key to Team Performance, we'll only address a few points in this section.

First and foremost, the goal is to build the capability of the *team* and then its members. Obviously, to a large degree the team's capability is a function of the individual skill sets of its members. However, far too often, managers think in terms of building each individual's skills without thinking how they fit into the overall needs of the team.

A better approach is for the team to first identify its needs and then determine where the gaps lie. That would then dictate how the individual employee training would be set up—based on the team's needs.

A skills matrix does just that. Such a grid pinpoints what the team needs in terms of overall capability, which then leads to the design of integrated team and individual development plans. (For an example of a skills matrix, see Chapter 5, Figure 5-5.) It also prompts the team to identify its capability needs, which then leads the team to identify where its weaknesses are.

Once that has been accomplished, it is time to take a more detailed look at the individual development needs of team members. This is where the supervisor or eventually the team itself would sit down with each team member and jointly develop an individual development plan (IDP) with the person. The IDP should identify the person's strengths and weaknesses, determine what type of development is needed, and then list a formal development plan.

One of the ongoing problems with IDPs is that a good plan is often written and then it's not looked at again until it is time to put together a new one. Such an approach is not only a waste of everyone's time; it also breeds cynicism because employees quickly recognize that the plan is merely an exercise in futility and won't be treated seriously. If that is the case, better to not even go down this path.

However, if you are serious about having a systematic approach for building capability within your team, then using IDPs may be the way to go, especially if these plans will be reviewed during performance appraisal feedback sessions. In this way, capability development and performance management are clearly linked, and everyone is able to see that the team is committed to improving skill sets in a systematic manner.

MANAGING THE DISENGAGEMENT OR DESELECTION OF TEAM MEMBERS

This process has two different components: 1) managing people who voluntarily leave your team and 2) managing people who involuntarily leave your team.

Naturally, the first process is the more pleasant of the two. People may voluntarily leave your team because they've accepted another job within the organization, retired, or resigned (e.g., for personal reasons or because they're moving out of town or going back to school). In this situation, the process often involves recognizing the team member's contribution to both your team and the organization. This may be accomplished in part by providing the employee with a plaque, gift, and/or certificate formally honoring the employee's service.

In many cases, it also involves some form of a ceremony and/or party, with the individual's accomplishments being recognized and other team members telling stories about working with their departing coworker. On some occasions, especially where the employee worked for an extended period of time, your team may even invite the employee's family to attend the event. These types of occasions celebrate the good work of an individual that is exiting the team and also foster a sense of family within the team. Along these lines, it is always a good idea to record these events either through photographs and/or videos and then post them or show them in a different forum. In this way, the team can relive them and reinforce all the goodwill that the event brought to the table.

When done right, such occasions set the right tone by conveying to everyone that each team member is important, which helps to establish a positive culture that will continue even after the team member departs. When you build a bond between team members that lasts after someone leaves, with team members staying in touch for years to come, the result may be access to people with valuable institutional memory, even if they no longer work there.

Beyond ceremonies, your team needs processes in place to ensure that knowledge is transferred from exiting members to others still on the team. This knowledge transfer can be accomplished in several ways. For example, the departing team member should work with the person who will be replacing her to ensure that the new employee is prepared for upcoming tasks. She should also ensure that well-written standard operating procedures (SOPs) are in place to guide her replacement in assuming his new roles and responsibilities.

Your team should have the off-boarding team member fill out a formal, written exit interview so that remaining team members can learn from her experiences and find out what they can do better. The team should also meet with her and engage in an honest dialogue as to how things went and how they can be improved. The results of these two interactions should be analyzed in order to identify areas that need to be addressed.

When team members need to involuntarily leave the team, a process needs to be in place to take action against poor performers and/or people who misbehave. Of course, the primary objective should not be to terminate the employee, but to turn him around; after all, the organization and your team invest an enormous amount of time, energy, and money in each team member, and you want to get a good return on that investment.

However, if the employee is unable or unwilling to improve, and you have made a good faith effort to try and help the employee, you need to take action to dismiss the employee. If you do not, you will severely damage the morale within your team. Other team members do not want to come to work every day, give it their best, and then helplessly watch an unproductive team member moan and groan while not pulling his weight.

The best way to handle a poor employee is during the probationary period (assuming the organization has one), which is really part of the selection process. Probation is your team's opportunity to assess whether the employee is a good fit for the job and, if not, to deselect him at this point. Otherwise, in many (although certainly not all) organizations, especially government, once the employee passes probation he has additional rights, which may make termination more difficult to accomplish later.

Initially, this is a role that rests squarely with management, and most team members will greatly respect a supervisor who is willing to stand up and do the right thing, even though it is often painful and time-consuming. Eventually, when your team moves closer to Stage Five, this role will likely be absorbed by some form of a team-based disciplinary board.

One of the keys to terminating a poor employee is to have well-defined processes for terminating individuals. Such processes should be spelled out in an internal statement and/or handbook that include policy guidance, sample letters, and perhaps even a table of penalties.

Whether the employee leaves voluntarily or involuntarily, there needs to be a process in place that ensures the transition goes smoothly. As such, we recommend that you provide outgoing employees with a list of human resources management (HRM) requirements, the appropriate documents they need to fill out, and instructions on how to actually complete the forms. These materials will minimize confusion about the process and ensure that the process goes as effectively and efficiently as possible.

CHALLENGES, TENSIONS, AND KEY FACTORS DURING IMPLEMENTATION

The biggest challenge here will probably be the process mapping/analysis—which, if done correctly, could involve a lot of upfront work. To mitigate these concerns, one approach would be to start off by mapping those team processes that are giving you the most trouble. In other words, concentrate your energies on the areas that are likely to provide you with the biggest bang for your buck.

With respect to the other team processes, they are all HRM-related and relatively easy to implement, with the exception being involuntarily off-boarding those individuals who are problem employees. One of the challenges is that some of these processes may need to be handled by HRM, so the team may not have full autonomy to implement them. As a result, we recommend that the team first determine how it would like these processes to work, in a manner that would support the team's transitioning to Stage Five and in a way that incorporates best practices (cited earlier in this chapter). Then the team can work with the powers that be to make the appropriate adjustments.

Involuntarily off-boarding problem team members is often difficult, even for supervisors, let alone a self-directed team. However, it is also absolutely necessary for your continued success.

For example, we once worked with a team of ten people who struggled to meet their goals. The problem was that two dysfunctional team members spent so much of their time complaining and documenting everything their supervisor did that they were not focused on the job and were pulling the team down. When the two were finally off-boarded, the team was left with only eight members, yet was able to achieve all the team goals. That is why sometimes you have to follow the principle of addition by subtraction.

The key is to build the off-boarding expertise into the team in a clear and consistent manner. Use HRM professionals to help teach your team the rules and set up the appropriate mechanisms/procedures. In addition, have both the HRM professionals and the team leader provide advice and assistance to the team where needed.

HOW IMPROVING YOUR PROCESSES WILL HELP BUILD LEADERS

As we have stated repeatedly in this book, the more your team's design choices are properly aligned, the more likely you will produce a team of leaders. One of the most important set of choices relates to your team's processes. The team's core work processes should be lean and efficient and help produce your team's desired results. Every employee should be intimately aware of these processes and, as a potential leader within the team, be willing to change these processes when necessary.

All your HRM processes should also be aligned with the goal of creating leaders. For example, the selecting, on-boarding and capability-building processes should be designed to develop future leaders. Moreover, the team's off-boarding process should manage the voluntary exit of team members in a manner consistent with the team's values; you also must be able to separate from the team members who either cannot or will not perform as leaders.

As we have shown you, having the right processes in place can make an enormous difference in the way your team evolves under the Five-Stage Team Development Model.

CHAPTER 4

Team Value Creation Model

Key principle: People are much more likely to become leaders if they understand the value they contribute to the team.

JACK STACK, A SUCCESSFUL business leader and author of the bestselling book *The Great Game of Business,*[1] tells the following story:

I got a call a few months ago from a friend who owns an architectural-engineering firm. He was upset because his company, which was doing about $3.3 million in sales, wasn't making money. His biggest concern was the $300,000 in debt he was carrying. Somehow, he said, he had to get people focused on generating profit so he could pay down the debt, or he would be forced to make deep cuts in the organization.

"Why wouldn't you want to get them focused on paying down the debt?" I asked.

"I figure the debt is my problem," he said.

My friend isn't unusual. Most managers think it's their job to deal with the big problems. So they shoulder those burdens alone, and the problems almost always get worse.

The reason is simple. To be successful in business, you have to be going somewhere, and everyone involved in getting you there has to know where it is. That's a basic rule, a higher law, but most companies miss it. They miss the fact that you have a much better chance of winning if everyone knows what it takes to win.[2]

That is why your team needs a team value creation model—it will provide you with the information you need to win.

For your team to run as a self-contained business, with everyone being a leader, everyone must know his or her success in creating value for the organization. And for people to know their success in creating value for the organization, they must have two vital pieces of information: their *cost* for the process/team, and the *value* of the output they produce. Calculating these two figures is not always easy. After all, our accounting practices do not usually yield this data without some creative number crunching. We will show you how to perform the requisite calculations in the second section of this chapter.

The cost of the team and the value of its output are the basic components of a team value creation model. By definition, such a model demonstrates and facilitates the creation of value in the production and/or delivery of a product or service.

With these two figures built into a model and some basic business management skills, you can determine how much value the team and each team member generates. This information will ensure that team members understand their value and will prod the team to look at its outputs and processes from a more practical, business-driven perspective. Moreover, it will help identify weaknesses within your team and suggest opportunities for productivity and efficiency improvements.

That is exactly what the team value creation model can do for you. It can help get the employees involved in knowing their value and learning what it takes to win.

Before we discuss the model in detail, let's provide the context within which the model should operate.

CONTEXT FOR VALUE-CREATING TEAMS

Value-creating teams function best in an organizational environment that supports them in running their mini-businesses. We know from the OSD Model for Teams that organizational elements must be aligned if we are going to get the results that we want. A value creation model is just one system, albeit a vital system that will allow you to thrive. Other important design elements include the structure of your team, the way you do your work, your goals, the information system that delivers wealth/ value creation data to you, the skills and competencies of team members, your reward system, and the shared values of the organization that support the notion of value-creating teams. These are, in essence, the elements of the OSD Model for Teams.

We are not going to address each of these areas in detail as we have already covered them in earlier chapters. However, it is important to make a few key points about these areas in order to reinforce how they relate to the value creation model.

STRUCTURE

The most important feature of the wealth-creating team structure is that your team should be organized around a distinct output that can be measured. Ideally, your team should be organized around the complete business process (i.e., end-to-end). But the amount of expertise required in such a case may cause the size of your team to be unwieldy, so your team should consider organizing itself around state changes, which we discussed in Chapter 3. One of the benefits of state changes is that they typically have clear inputs, throughputs, and outputs.

The reason for organizing around a state change or a group of state changes is to identify your team's output. After all, if your team does not have a distinct output, it certainly will not be able to make or account for improvements to that output—and continuous improvement is an essential characteristic of wealth-creating teams.

The number of state changes within your team's domain is determined by the patterns of variability in the product. Variances, or defects, are generally observed downstream from where they originally occur. If your team owns a complete state change or several complete state changes, it will be more aware of the downstream impact of variances. That is why we conduct a technical analysis—to help uncover where concentrations of variability occur, suggesting natural boundaries for teams.

For example, some years ago we had the privilege of working with a wonderful team of leasing professionals. When examining their work process through a state change perspective, we found that 80 percent of the variances occurred in the "receive a request for financing" subprocess or state change. Most of the variances had to do with the availability, accuracy, and completeness of the applicants' legal entity, location, credit history, and bank information. These variances had a huge impact on the credit process as well as the downstream collections process.

The problem was driven to a large extent by the fact that three different departments performed three key processes. Understanding the principle of minimizing the transference of variances from one work team to another and controlling the variances at the source, they were able to organize around specific customer segment teams owning the request for financing, credit, contracts, customer service, and collections processes. This design helped drive a powerful value-creating team.

GOALS

Value-creating team members must be focused on a set of team goals, but they must also know how these goals relate to overall organizational results. Knowledge of these goals goes hand in hand with the development and use of appropriate information systems.

INFORMATION

As we mentioned in the last chapter, it is critical for your team to know its goals and to have frequent, timely information about the progress it is making. First and foremost, the information must be about results at the process, subprocess, and team level, and it must be given to the team directly—to the people who need to make decisions about their own results.

Second, the information must be delivered frequently. Just like in sports, whether bowling, baseball, or the Olympics, individuals as well as teams want to know how they are doing. After all, according to Jack Stack, everyone likes a game.

"Gamesmanship lies at the heart of Stack's approach to management," according to *Inc. Magazine.* "Virtually everything that happens at SRC [the company Stack founded] is based on the premise that business is essentially a game—one, moreover, that almost anyone can learn to play. As with most games, however, people won't bother to learn it unless they 'get' it. That means, first, they must understand the rules; second, they must receive enough information to let them follow the action; and third, they must have the opportunity to win or lose."[3]

We have found that a daily value creation model gives teams a strong sense of accomplishment. The rate at which information on results (costs, output, and value) is available—hourly, daily, or weekly—should determine how often the team gets this information.

Third, the information must be delivered on a timely basis. It is useless for your team to know its results a month afterward. Team members must be able to connect the experience of producing the output with data about the cost and quality of that output, so that they can self-correct. Particularly when rewards are tied to results, your team members will want to correct their course as soon as possible.

Having this kind of information available to your team is absolutely crucial, even if it means making calculations by hand. In fact, it is a travesty to ask your team to be self-managing without giving it information. It is like asking people to make decisions absent any data.

Without information about your business, the team is likely to fall into a quagmire of interpersonal difficulties and empty blaming. Give your team members the information, and with a little training they will use it to the tremendous benefit of the team and the company.

SKILLS AND COMPETENCIES

Running a business requires skills that many team members have never been required to develop. But with some training and coaching from their team leader, they can learn the needed competencies.

First, using the model, they must be able to determine if they created value for the company and, if so, how much. They must be able to determine which of the operational data given them is most relevant.

Second, they must have meeting management skills (among other business management skills). Most important, they must have norms in place to bring up problems highlighted by the data they receive. They must also be able to run and participate in team meetings where they bring up problems and identify gaps between current performance and target performance.

Third, they should have problem-solving skills. They must have a roadmap to follow to go offline, analyze data, make recommendations, and implement solutions.

What we want to avoid is having your team trained in meeting management skills, problem-solving skills, and interpersonal communications skills without any useful data about your business to leverage in utilizing these skills.

REWARDS

If your team wants to take over daily management functions and run itself like a mini-business, it needs to have rewards connected to how well it manages its results. You should offer rewards at both the team and individual levels.

SHARED VALUES

A set of shared values is crucial to the effectiveness of your team. First of all, the organization must not only allow, but also expect your team to take the time, on a daily or weekly basis, to review your results and identify gaps. Otherwise, your team may become stymied if it is unable to get together and evaluate its performance.

Second, your organizational and team climate must encourage members to bring up problems. If they are afraid to speak up for any reason, wealth generation will be limited and innovation and creativity will be discouraged.

Third, team members must be free to suggest changes. Having the information, skills, and freedom to analyze problems is hardly useful if recommendations cannot be implemented. Undoubtedly, most team recommendations for change should be fact-based. If a cost/benefit analysis is beyond the scope of the team, then the results of that analysis should be clearly communicated to them.

If your team or organization's cost/benefit analysis indicates that a change is in order, then the organization must support all data-driven change recommendations. Leaders must be willing to allow the team to change schedules, technology, procedures, and other design elements that have impact upon it. The organization must teach your team that it is truly free to make changes, based on data or facts, in order to improve your results.

DEVELOPING A TEAM VALUE CREATION MODEL

As stated earlier, to develop an individualized team model, your team members need two basic pieces of information: the *cost* for the process/organization and the *value* of the output they produce.

COST

The cost of each person should be a fully allocated cost. It should include salary, benefits, and any other associated costs.

A good place to find this information is in an operating statement that is stratified down to the team level. An operating statement is a financial statement that gives operating results for a specific period. Figure 4-1 is a sample operating statement.

As you can see in this example, year-to-date (YTD), the team has cost the organization $297,757 and has spent 43 percent of its budget. For the past month, it spent $77,344.

In order to deeply understand all of its costs, the team members need to know what is included in the applicable categories on the statement (see the left-hand column of Figure 4-1, under Summary by Account.) For example, under Salaries and Wages, here are the appropriate definitions of the line items (bear in mind that definitions may be slightly different from organization to organization):

- Salaries are fixed compensation periodically paid to a person for regular work or services.

- Wages are money that is paid to a person for work or services, as by the hour, day, or week.

FIGURE 4-1. Sample operating statement for a team.

As of June 30, 2012

	Actuals		Budget			
	Current Month	YTD	Amount	% Spent	Budget Balance	Projected Annual %
Total by Team	**$77,344**	**$297,767**	**$691,409**	**43%**	**$393,653**	**86%**
Summary by Account						
Salaries and Wages	$56,861	$215,000	$453,936	47%	$238,936	95%
Salaries and Wages - OT	$1,444	$2,386	$5,000	48%	$2,614	95%
Salaries and Wages - Temp	$0	$0	$30,000	0%	$30,000	0%
Salaries and Wages	**$58,305**	**$217,386**	**$488,936**	**44%**	**$271,550**	**89%**
Social Security	$4,244	$15,907	$36,327	44%	$20,420	88%
Retirement Program	$3,822	$14,966	$32,396	46%	$17,430	92%
Retirement Savings	$1,776	$7,998	$12,246	65%	$4,248	131%
Medical Insurance Program	$8,536	$33,534	$74,367	45%	$40,833	90%
Rewards	$0	$0	$1,070	0%	$1,070	0%

FIGURE 4-1. Sample operating statement for a team. (continued)

Employee Benefits	**$18,380**	**$72,405**	**$156,406**	**46%**	**$84,001**	**93%**
Travel - Mileage Reimbursement	$0	$0	$750	0%	$750	0%
Travel Expenses	-	-	**$750**	**0%**	**$750**	**0%**
Operating Material Supplies	$0	$0	$750	0%	$750	0%
Materials and Supplies	-	-	**$750**	**0%**	**$750**	**0%**
Telephone	$659	$7,950	$42,917	19%	$34,967	37%
Luncheons and Social	$0	$0	$1,650	0%	$1,650	0%
Books and Film	$0	$17	$0	0%	-$17	0%
General Administrative	$659	$7,967	$44,567	18%	$36,600	36%
Total Expense	**$77,344**	**$297,757**	**$691,409**	**43%**	**$393,652**	**86%**
Allocations						
Revenue						
Total	**$77,344**	**$297,757**	**$691,409**	**43%**	**$393,652**	**86%**

- Overtime is extra time worked before or after one's regularly scheduled working hours.

- Temporary means salary paid to temporary employees or contractors.

For Employee Benefits (which are sometimes referred to as Wage Burden), listed below are the definitions:

- Social Security is taxes paid into the federally mandated Social Security program on the team member's behalf.

- Retirement Program and Savings is money contributed to retirement programs, such as 401(k)s or pensions.

- Medical Insurance is money paid toward medical insurance.

- Rewards means money paid out to team members in the form of rewards and recognition.

The remaining categories on the left-hand side of the operating statement in Figure 4-1 are broken down into Travel Expenses, Materials and Supplies, and General Administrative. They include airfare, meals, lodging, telephones, books, computers, printers, and office furniture. These three categories can also be grouped into one overall category of Discretionary Spending because they all involve funds that can be used at the team's discretion, at least under this scenario. Purchases under Discretionary Spending may be made through a company credit card, a direct charge, or an invoice, as appropriate.

Moving to our right at the top of the operating statement, the next broad category covers Actuals, which represent what the team actually spent for each account or operating statement line item. For the team, this is the equivalent of its "checkbook."

Moving farther to the right is the team's Budget. This is the amount of money set aside for each account or line item in the operating statement. Phrased differently, it is a plan for how much the team will spend each month, quarter, and year. Note that in this area in Figure 4-1, the budgeted amount per line item, the percentage of that amount spent, and the balance remaining are all shown.

The last column on the right is the Projected Annual Percentage. This percentage is what the team projects it will spend if it continues for the remainder of the year at its current rate of spending.

DIRECT COSTS VS. INDIRECT COSTS

In order to build the team value creation model, your team also needs to identify what its direct and indirect costs are. You need to ensure that *all* the team's costs are included in the calculations that determine the value the team is creating and whether it is making a profit or a loss.

Direct costs are directly related to the delivery of a transaction or service (e.g., cost of customer service agents).

Overhead costs that cannot be directly attributed to the delivery of a service (e.g., management) are indirect costs.

Let's look at an example of how both types of costs could be applied to the team value creation model. In this simplified example, the salary, wages, and benefits of each team equal $100,000. One manager oversees two teams, referred to as Team 1 and Team 2. The manager's salary and benefits equate to $50,000. One-half of the manager's salary and benefits are added to each team's direct costs (resulting in a total of $125,000 being allocated per team).

Direct Costs

Team 1: Cost to Support Customer A: $100,000

Team 2: Cost to Support Customer A: $100,000

Indirect Costs or Overhead

Team 1: ½ Cost of Manager: $25,000

Team 2: ½ Cost of Manager: $25,000

Fully Burdened or Direct and Indirect Costs

Team 1: Direct + Indirect Costs $125,000

Team 2: Direct + Indirect Costs $125,000

VALUE

Perhaps the single most important component of the team value creation model is determining what the *value* of the team's output is. We need to compare the value of the team's output relative to its overall costs to determine whether it is making a profit or incurring a loss.

The value of the team's output can be determined in a number of ways:

1. By the market value for the team's output—that is, the price somebody (a customer, another department, or division) is willing to pay for that output

2. By the price the team would pay another group for the output (a "make or buy" decision)

3. By industry best practice metrics

4. By the total cost currently incurred divided by the number of units produced to make that output

5. By internal metrics or cost structure (activity-based costing)

Teams that are aware of their markets should have immediate access to at least some of this information. For example, you should know what a competitor charges to produce a similar transaction. Through benchmarking, you should know what the industry standard is for the work you do. You should also be aware of what the going rate is to outsource that work.

You can also develop information about value through environmental scans, which may include focus groups. The more information you have regarding value in the marketplace, the easier it will be for you to assign a value to a particular transaction for the purposes of the model.

Let's look at an example where we use a simple calculation to determine the value of a transaction. Under this scenario, we take an activity-based cost approach to calculating value:

$$\frac{\text{Cost of Transactions}}{\text{Number of Transactions}} = \text{Cost per Transaction}$$

For this example, let's assume that the team spent $10,000 to produce 500 transactions during a fixed period of time. Using the previous formula, the cost per transaction would be $20, as follows:

$$\frac{\$10,000}{500} \ = \ \$20$$

Using the team's value creation model (which we will go over next), the team would compare the value per transaction (in this case $20) relative to the new actual cost per transaction to determine whether positive or negative value is created.

Note that the team could also assign different values or weights to its transactions based on the degree of complexity of each transaction. For example, you might weight complex transactions at $30, while easy ones might only be worth $10, depending on the time and costs used to complete both transactions. We recommend this weighted approach because it will provide a more accurate picture of the value produced. In addition, it will also encourage team members to work a mix of cases and not simply focus on the easiest transactions because they will receive the appropriate degree of credit for each. (Remember, you get what you design for.)

SAMPLE MODEL

Now that we have discussed the basic components of the team value creation model, let's see what one would actually look like.

As you can see, the model in Figure 4-2 lists the employees in the far left column, although for the purposes of this example, they are

FIGURE 4-2. Sample team value creation model for a pay period.

Em	Avg Hrly Wage	Hrs	Total Salary Cost	Burden to Apply	Total Wage Burden Cost	Section Expense (Actual)	Sect OH	Div OH	Total Wage w/ OH Cost	Total Type 1	Value Type 1	Total Type 2	Value Type 2	Total Value Created	Ind. (+) or (-) Value
1	$12.3	80	$ 980.0	32.0%	$1,293.6	$122.0	$156	$213	$1,784.6	300	$5.21	180	$4.56	$2,383.8	$599.2
2	$12.3	40	$ 490.0	32.0%	$646.8	$122.0	$156	$213	$1,137.8	152	$5.21	72	$4.56	$1,120.2	-$17.6
3	$12.3	80	$ 980.0	32.0%	$1,293.6	$122.0	$156	$213	$1,784.6	320	$5.21	65	$4.56	$1,963.6	$179.0
4	$12.3	80	$ 980.0	32.0%	$1,293.6	$122.0	$156	$213	$1,784.6	280	$5.21	155	$4.56	$2,165.6	$381.0
5	$12.3	36	$ 441.0	32.0%	$582.1	$122.0	$156	$213	$1,073.1	175	$5.21	102	$4.56	$1,376.9	$303.8
6	$12.3	42	$ 514.5	32.0%	$679.1	$122.0	$156	$213	$1,170.1	249	$5.21	60	$4.56	$1,570.9	$400.8
7	$12.3	77	$ 943.3	32.0%	$1,245.1	$122.0	$156	$213	$1,736.1	285	$5.21	56	$4.56	$1,740.2	$4.1
8	$12.3	80	$ 980.0	32.0%	$1,293.6	$122.0	$156	$213	$1,784.6	210	$5.21	35	$4.56	$1,253.7	-$530.9
9	$12.3	80	$ 980.0	32.0%	$1,293.6	$122.0	$156	$213	$1,784.6	240	$5.21	58	$4.56	$1,514.9	-$269.7
10	$12.3	45	$ 551.3	32.0%	$727.7	$122.0	$156	$213	$1,218.7	162	$5.21	100	$4.56	$1,300.0	$81.4
Totals			$ 7,840		$10,348.8	$1,220	$1,560	$2,130	$15,259	2,373		883		$16,390	$1,131

Notes:
To make this document easier to read, some figures are rounded to one or zero decimal places.
"Em" means "Employees."
"PP" means "Pay Period."
"Section Expense (Actual)" refers to the team's discretionary expenses that are apportioned to each team member's costs.
"Sect" means "Section."
"Div" means "Division."
"OH" means "Overhead."
"Total Type 1 and 2" refers to the total number of contacts made per type.

identified by a number (i.e., Employee 1, Employee 2, etc.). Next to this is each employee's hourly wage, the number of hours they worked, and then the total salary, which is simply the hourly wage multiplied by the number of hours worked (shown as total salary.) Note that the total salary costs for the team during the pay period was $7,840.

The next two columns include a fixed percentage multiplier (32 percent) for Wage Burden or Employee Benefits, which when multiplied by the total Salary, brings the total Salary and Wage Burden costs to $10,348.80. See column 6—"Total Wage Burden Cost"—in Figure 4-2.

Continuing to move left to right, we then add one-tenth of the Discretionary Expenses ($1,220) to the cost for each employee and the total amount to the team. We then do the same thing for Overhead, which includes a percentage of section management ($1,560) and division management ($2,130) and spread that amount equally across all teams in a section. This provides us with the Total Wages with Overhead Costs by employee and for the team ($15,259), which represents the total costs for the team for the pay period. See column 10—"Total Wage w/OH Cost"— in Figure 4-2.

The next few columns show the number of transactions (referred to here as "contacts") for two different types of transactions. (Remember, we earlier recommended measuring more than one type of transaction if different transactions varied significantly in complexity.) To the right of the number of the transaction type completed is the value assigned to each (i.e., $5.21 for Type 1 contacts and $4.56 for Type 2 contacts). These values could have been developed using the cost per transaction formula given previously in this chapter or by using one of several other methods. The best and most credible way to capture the number of transactions completed by the team is through some form of a system-generated report, such as the phone system.

We then determine the total value created by multiplying the number of transactions completed by their value and comparing the value created to the total cost. This calculation will determine whether the team and each team member have created a positive or a negative value. See the last column—"Ind. Positive (+) or Negative (-) Value"—in Figure 4-2.

In this example, note that while the team had an increase in value of $1,131 for the pay period, which is good, three members (Employees 2, 8, and 9) operated at a loss. Had they too had an increase, the team's overall increase would have almost doubled. Clearly, the team needs to focus on these three individuals and bring them up to snuff.

A good example of a successful team value creation model occurred at an organization that instituted a value creation model as a foundation element. The organization wanted to look at the cost of a put-on (or a securities trade), which involves a request for financing, a determination of credit worthiness, and the appropriate rate, all the way until it becomes an asset that is placed on the company's books.

At the time, the organization was experiencing problems with the contractor who was doing this work for them, so the organization's managers took over the work, decided to perform it in-house, and created their own model. In addition to having quality issues with the vendor, they learned it had been costing them $230 to complete one put-on.

They then decided to find out who was best in class in this industry. Through benchmarking, they found someone who could perform a put-on for $120. Since the organization's leaders were determined to keep the work in-house, they decided that $120 was too demoralizing as an initial goal for their own teams to meet, so they started with a value of $210 per put-on. From there, they kept whittling down the value to $190, then $170, then $150. Eventually, they got the value of the put-on down to $95, which created a cost separation from them and the rest of the industry and real bottom-line value creation.

The point here is that management didn't blindly set up the model. It used sound judgment in determining the value of a put-on for teams that had never used a value creation model and allowed the team to develop and get into the game. When it comes to determining value, sometimes the lowest number is the right number and sometimes it is not.

With the team value creation model now developed, your team can begin to operate as a mini-business. For the first time, it will have the same type of information that senior leaders have with respect to increase or decrease of value in order to make key decisions that affect everyone's destiny. Your team members will be able to ask the tough questions and address them, *before* upper management gets involved. Not only that, team members will also be able to have some fun because they will now be part of the game.

So how do you get started?

To build and utilize a team value creation model, we recommend that your team take the following steps:

1. Get a template with pre-populated fields.

2. Also get the following reports:

    - Human resources/finance payroll report (hours only)

    - A system-generated list containing the number of transactions per employee/team

- The percentage of monthly section and division overhead

- Value by transaction type (which the team determines as described earlier in Figure 4-2)

3. Determine the frequency of reports to be generated—daily, weekly, or monthly, although daily is preferred.

4. Hold meetings to discuss options for increasing value.

5. Develop and share a team continuous process improvement plan.

Here is a list of brainstorming questions your team should ask whenever it is reviewing the results of the model:

- Is performance consistent across the team? Why or why not?

- How do we compare to other teams? Are there best practices to be shared?

- What are our strengths or areas for improvement?

- Are resources scheduled effectively?

- Are we using our manager effectively?

- Is there a way to streamline customer service/support procedures?

- Are there any policies or rules that we don't understand that may get in our way?

Once your team members become comfortable with the value creation model, they will ask themselves, "How did we ever get along without it?" The model is an extremely valuable tool for managing the team, improving its value to the organization, and becoming more engaged in the day-to-day operations of the team.

A WHOLE-BRAINED APPROACH

For your team to truly succeed, it must take a whole-brained approach to managing the team operation. That is, while team members must know how they are doing and whether they are creating an increase or decrease in value for the organization, at the same time, they must also be connected around a sense of purpose.

In our experience and research, we have found that the best teams do both. They focus on both the collective left brain (the logical, analytical side) and right brain (the purposeful, value-based holistic, emotional side)[4] in order to achieve the team's maximum potential. Framed differently, you should rally your team members around your mission *and* your metrics, and incorporate males and females, introverts and extroverts, Republicans, Democrats, and Independents, artists and technicians. When this happens, your team will be truly optimizing its human potential and the results can be stunning.

CHALLENGES, TENSIONS, AND KEY FACTORS DURING IMPLEMENTATION

The first challenge is making sure that everyone on the team understands why you are implementing the model. Once that is clear, people will need to learn where the underlying information comes from and what each data point means. This will not be an easy thing for everyone to grasp; however, it is definitely worth the time it will take to teach all the team members about it.

Another key challenge is that not everyone may want the entire team to know how much value individuals are (or are not) contributing to the team. After all, there will likely be significant differences in performance between team members, and this information may cause some fear and insecurity. Moreover, working in an environment where this kind of information is transparent to all can be threatening to low performers.

On the other hand, expect most of the other team members to welcome the concept since they will be proud to see how much value they contribute and they will want to know who the outliers are so that they can take steps to ensure everyone gets up to snuff—which is exactly what you want to have happen. That is, you want to create an environment where team members work together to help each other and produce as much value as possible.

Your team will also have to weigh the following question: With everything required to transform the team, when is the best time to develop and implement the model? We believe the answer is that the model is something that should be accomplished early in the process, because once the team understands its underlying principles and practices, the model is relatively easy to build. More important, it will help jump-start your team's progress toward self-management as the team will look at performance and value creation in a new and exciting way.

HOW DEVELOPING A VALUE CREATION MODEL WILL HELP BUILD LEADERS

When the information from the model suddenly becomes available, it will quickly elevate the team and get everyone in the game. Instead of seeing themselves as merely workers who do what they are told, the model will prompt team members to look at what they and the team contribute to the bottom line.

Probably for the first time in their careers, they will examine their work from the perspective of a leader. They will see how much value they are creating and wonder how they can add more. They will look more deeply at their inputs, outputs, and outcomes and ask each other if there are better ways to do things. They will even start comparing their contributions to other competitors, including the best in class, and start thinking outside the box.

This is exactly the way you want your team and its members to think—like leaders. Our experience is that this powerful tool becomes a way of thinking for each team member. Moreover, your team members will take this knowledge and apply it in their other roles and help their family and friends learn and apply it, too.

Developing and Managing Knowledge Is Key to Team Performance

Key principle: To build leaders, you must determine the knowledge they need, decide how to acquire it, and then manage its distribution.

WE HAVE SPENT A lot of time so far showing you how to examine—through process analysis—the work in your team that is crucial but not sufficient to design a team that can deliver. You must also look at the *knowledge* required to create value for customers.

Technologies, processes, economic conditions, and customer requirements all change incessantly, but what remains constant is the tremendous power of the minds of the people on your team—to generate new ideas, share them, and convert them into value for customers. It is said that knowledge is the purest source of advantage for high-performing teams. To deliver that extraordinary value, teams must manage the speed of discovery and diffusion of key knowledge better than any other alternative source.

It is especially important to recognize that the diffusion and application of fresh ideas are inherently *social* activities. How well your team uses knowledge is dependent on the quality and extent of the social networks within and surrounding the team.

Therefore, you should use the culture analysis tool set (as described in Chapter 3) to study knowledge, networks, and culture in your team. Using information from your process analysis, you can seek to understand what knowledge is distinctive and determine how well that knowledge is being converted into customer value. Culture analysis will also look at how well your team renews its knowledge base. In other words, you will study your team's learning capability.

You will also study the networks surrounding critical roles in your team. Knowledge, by its very nature, cannot be shared outside the context of active, trusting, cooperative relationships—the right people talking to the right people about the right things at the right time. Innovation and team improvement rarely spring from isolated individual efforts, so we perform a culture analysis to identify new ways to encourage the purposeful seeking and sharing of critical knowledge.

Before we walk you through the culture analysis tool set in more detail, it is important to reflect on what we have learned about learning. Our research has found that:

- We need to focus learning on performance capabilities.
- Knowledge diffusion and deployment are harder than discovery.
- If we don't manage what we learn, we forget it or can't find it.
- We need to find ways to dramatically increase learning capabilities (i.e., knowledge development capabilities).[1]

These are the principles that govern our approach to learning, and they are why we have developed the cultural analysis tools that we share with you now. They have been carefully designed as part of an overall and integrated package that will enable you to optimally acquire, assess, diffuse, and deploy knowledge throughout your team, with the goal always being outstanding performance by creating a team of leaders.

CULTURAL ANALYSIS: KNOWLEDGE MANAGEMENT

Chapter 3 discussed the components of the cultural analysis, including but not limited to those that relate to knowledge management. Some of these components were described more than others, such as the interaction network analysis (a means of assessing the communication patterns and networks within a team/organization) and the individual needs assessments. As a result, we won't repeat that discussion here.

The next tool that we use is the voice of the team assessment. This survey determines the extent to which members of a team display the behaviors, feelings, and attributes required to drive the team to its desired outcomes. We ask each team member to assess a series of statements, ranking each on a scale of 1 to 5, with 1 meaning "to a very small extent" and 5 meaning "to a very large extent." As examples, consider these statements:

- The people I work with understand our mission and vision.

- The people I work with clearly understand what is important to each of our customers.

- Teamwork is encouraged and we always work as a team.

- My teammates are committed to doing a good job.

- We work toward specific and measurable goals that are well understood by all members of our team.

This assessment gives an excellent picture of the "state of the team" from the perspective of each of its members. It clearly lays out how the team sees things from a variety of angles and helps the team to decide where it needs to go in terms of building knowledge, skill sets, and culture.

We next move on to a knowledge assessment, which links design choices about process changes, new structures, and other improvements with a corresponding development of beliefs, skills, and information.

The team knowledge (TK) needed to deliver outstanding performance (OP) includes tacit values, attitudes, and expertise. A design cannot be complete, nor can we be confident that it will be successful, until we consider the full range of team knowledge to achieve performance goals and make plans for developing that knowledge.

Figure 5-1 shows the various types of team knowledge. In general, *tacit* knowledge refers to knowledge that one has but cannot explain. It is difficult or impossible to put into words. *Codifiable* or *explicit* knowledge, on the other hand, is knowledge that can be explained and organized into rules or policies. *Know-that* refers to knowledge that is a fact or a truth, including an idea or a belief that's held as true. *Know-how* indicates the ability to perform tasks or operations either "in your head" or "in action."

More specifically, there are four types of team knowledge modeled in Figure 5-1:

FIGURE 5-1. Four types of team/organizational knowledge.

	Codifiable	Tacit
Know-That	Facts	Beliefs
Know-How	Routines	Expertise

1. *Codifiable know-that* includes data and information. In organizations, codifiable know-that is often embodied in memos, reports, and symbols.

2. *Codifiable know-how* includes procedures and routine skills that are often embedded in process charts, organization charts, policies, manuals, equipment, and the design of facilities.

3. *Tacit know-that* includes attitudes, values, intuitions, beliefs, and basic assumptions that are so complex, dynamic, or implicit that they resist codification.

4. *Tacit know-how* refers to complex skills that are highly developed yet little understood by the people who use them. It resists codification and explanation. It includes expertise and artistry.

Often, more than half of the knowledge in a team is tacit, and an even greater proportion of *the most valuable knowledge* in teams is tacit. Yet the tendency is to attend only to knowledge that is explicit.

High-performance teams are more conscious of tacit (noncodifiable) knowledge. It's almost Zen-like. If you have ever played basketball, you know that when the team is playing at a high level, it feels as though everyone knows what the other player is doing. They are in the flow and can anticipate each other's moves.

If you have played tennis and truly developed a feel for the game, you begin to do things instinctively. You quickly realize that it's one thing to learn the technical part of the game (i.e., the codifiable part): To have ample time to hit the ball, you must take your racquet back early; to hit with topspin, you must swing your racquet in a low to high motion; to serve properly, you must keep your left arm up for as long as possible and "scratch your back" with the racquet before accelerating up and over the ball. However, it's quite another thing to know when to really go for your shots, when to play more defensively, and when to come to the net. This is knowledge that is tacit and comes from experience and developing a sixth sense for the game.

Consider how complex the game of golf is. In a span of 1.5 seconds, you have to make a series of complicated but related moves—stay balanced, keep your hands soft, clear your hips, follow through—while at the same time staying focused, keeping relaxed, and maintaining your tempo. In short, this is close to impossible *unless* you have developed the requisite muscle memory or, framed differently, mastered the tacit part of the know-that and know-how.

Teams have the same struggle. They need to develop all types of knowledge and expertise so that it becomes second nature, thus enabling them to be able to make many rapid but sound decisions. The point here is that regardless of your sport or field, the best teams possess and capitalize on the tacit knowledge that helps differentiate them from their competitors.

You have probably codified much if not most of your explicit knowledge already in manuals and standard operating procedures. That is definitely a good thing. However, you are likely to underestimate the prevalence and importance of tacit knowledge unless you extend design work in that direction. Only when both kinds of knowledge—explicit and tacit—are recognized, developed, and aligned can performance results begin to approach their potential. There is simply no replacement for the tacit know-how of individuals and groups when it comes to managing processes and providing products and services.

All four types of team knowledge must be aligned and balanced. In other words, they must not contradict each other, and they must all be of the same relative strength. For example, if routines (codifiable know-how) are changed without a corresponding development of the expertise (tacit know-how) required to carry out those routines, performance outcomes will be compromised. Likewise, if new beliefs (tacit know-that) about the importance of customer service are developed, customer satisfaction outcomes still will lag if new performance management systems relating to customer service (codifiable know-that) are not put into place or are only weakly communicated.

Each type of knowledge is best developed by distinct types of team learning (TL) processes. Tacit knowledge is more likely to be developed with unstructured methods, while codifiable, explicit knowledge is learned best in conventional, structured settings. Know-that is learned just fine through cerebral methods such as study, conversations, and reflection, while know-how is best learned through action-oriented methods.

Figure 5-2 is a matrix that outlines possible learning methods for the different types of learning processes.

Finally, team conditions must be put into place that will foster learning. Team conditions are the design elements of the OSD processes, structure, and information systems. For example, Google encouraged its

FIGURE 5-2. Team learning methods.

	Structured	Unstructured
Cognition-based	■ Benchmarking ■ Customer research ■ Acquisition ■ Scanning ■ Reflection ■ Tours and reports ■ Training	■ Experience ■ Relationships ■ Personal communication ■ "Skip-level" dialogue ■ Storytelling ■ President's breakfast ■ All-company reviews
Action-based	■ Experimental behavior ■ Experiential learning ■ Documents manuscripts ■ Training ■ Videos ■ Recipes ■ Standardization ■ Personnel rotation	■ Expertise ■ Pilots ■ Action research ■ Alliances/joint ventures ■ Acquisitions ■ Experiential learning ■ Simulations ■ Apprenticeships ■ Personnel rotation

best and brightest to spend 10 percent of their time at work doing whatever they thought would benefit Google. At Hallmark, team members were requested to learn something new and to share it with someone else. Jack Welch of GE required members of his senior team to report what they had learned and whom they had in turn taught. Learning labs, learning rooms, and offsite retreats are other examples of design elements that can foster a learning environment.

CONDUCTING A KNOWLEDGE ASSESSMENT

With the background about team knowledge given in the last few pages, you can complete a Knowledge Assessment. This tool provides you with a wonderful opportunity to take a step back, look at the four knowledge types required by your team, and then put a plan together to meet your needs.

Here are the steps to follow:

1. Review your desired performance outcomes.

2. Identify the team "knowledge domains" essential to these outcomes. Knowledge domains are areas of capability in the organization that are linked to performance outcomes. They can be related to customers, products and services, technical processes, or administrative processes. For example, an insurance company might designate "claims processing" as an important knowledge domain related to its technical processes. A retail store might identify "inventory management" as a critical knowledge domain. An example of a knowledge domain linked to administrative processes is "team management," which is important to an organization with self-directed work teams.

3. For each knowledge domain, list its four types of knowledge: codifiable know-that, codifiable know-how, tacit know-that, and tacit know-how. Use a four-box organizational knowledge table.

4. For each type of knowledge, identify complementary learning methods to develop that knowledge. Use a four-box learning methods table.

5. Transfer any design choice ideas to a design ideas matrix. Use this matrix to record the ideas identified during your team design analysis (i.e., when analyzing the environment, the technical system, and the social system).

Figure 5-3 has templates that you can use for identifying the knowledge types needed for each domain and the related learning processes.

The learning processes assessment is a checkup of the processes in place to foster the development and diffusion of critical knowledge. In the first part of the knowledge assessment (Figure 5-3), you identified critical knowledge domains and the four types of knowledge associated with each one of the domains. You gave thought to the learning methods for acquiring each type of knowledge. The second part of the knowledge assessment examines the learning processes in your team and your ability to manage knowledge in all of these five ways:

1. *Acquire or create.* Your team must continuously acquire (from external or internal sources) know-that or know-how that is related to content, people, or equipment.

2. *Capture/codify.* Your team must strive to capture or codify this knowledge (i.e., document it or add it to the database).

3. *Disseminate.* Your team must effectively disseminate knowledge, either by standardizing processes or encouraging people to share new knowledge with others or, more formally, teach it.

4. *Apply.* Your team must be able to use knowledge effectively.

5. *Renew.* Your team must be able to unlearn obsolete knowledge or bring it up-to-date.

What is important is not just *what* knowledge is gained, but also *how widespread* that knowledge is held. A simple equation demonstrates this concept:

FIGURE 5-3. Knowledge assessment templates.

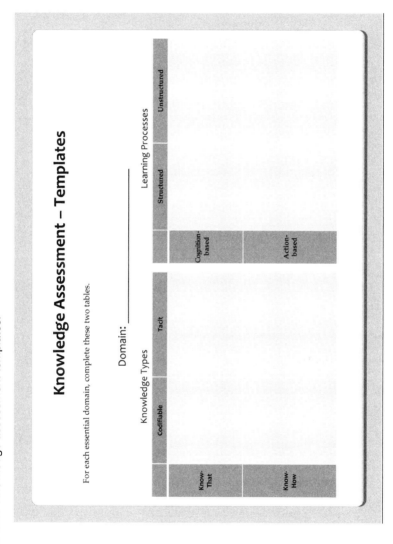

$$\text{Knowledge Capability (\textbf{KC})} \quad = \quad \textbf{D} \quad \times \quad \textbf{D}$$

$$\textbf{Knowledge Capability} \quad = \quad \textbf{Discovery} \quad \times \quad \textbf{Diffusion}$$

Where:

Discovery means inventing programs, products, processes, procedures, and learning how best to implement them.

Diffusion means sharing and applying the concepts of new products, programs, processes, as well as the know-how. The ability to implement must be shared/transferred as well.

GETTING AND SPREADING KNOWLEDGE

Most teams, when rating their ability to learn, rate their ability to *discover* new information much better than their ability to *diffuse* new discoveries throughout the team. For example, on a 10-point scale, where 10 means very able and 1 means unable, a team might give itself a 7 for the ability to discover and a 2 for the ability to diffuse:

$$KC \quad = \quad D \quad \times \quad D$$

$$14 \quad = \quad 7 \quad \times \quad 2$$

If your team targets improvement efforts at raising the discovery score by one point, it could raise its overall learning capability score to a 16:

$$KC \quad = \quad D \quad \times \quad D$$

$$14 \quad = \quad 7 \quad \times \quad 2 \text{ (current score)}$$

$$16 \quad = \quad 8 \quad \times \quad 2 \text{ (targeted score)}$$

But if the team can raise its diffusion score even one point, it can raise its overall score by 50 percent, to a 21. And if the team can raise the diffusion score to the level of the discovery score, the change in learning capability would be tremendous—a 250 percent improvement:

$$KC = D \times D$$

$$14 = 7 \times 2 \text{ (current score)}$$

$$21 = 7 \times 3 \text{ (targeted score)}$$

$$49 = 7 \times 7 \text{ (targeted score)}$$

By thinking about your team's ability to learn in this manner, you'll find that a surprising improvement can be secured if the team is effective at supporting the diffusion of intellectual capital across unit boundaries.

Here are the steps to take:

1. For all the essential knowledge domains, complete the knowledge assessment templates (see the templates shown in Figure 5-4).

2. Discuss organization conditions (systems and processes) that will foster or institutionalize the acquisition, creation, codification, diffusion, application, and renewal of organization knowledge.

3. Transfer design choice ideas to the team knowledge template.

SKILLS MATRIX

The final culture analysis tool that relates to knowledge management is the skills matrix, which outlines the skills and skill levels needed by a

FIGURE 5-4. Team knowledge template.

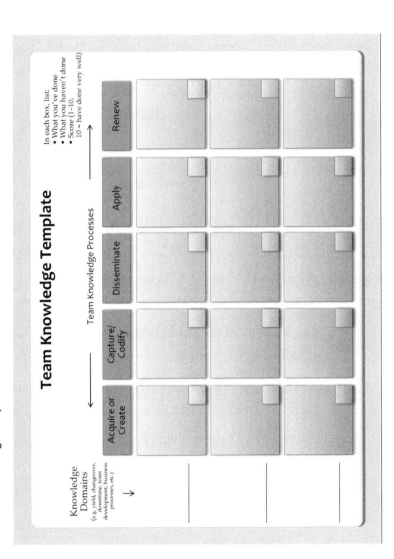

Team Knowledge Template

Knowledge
Domains
(e.g., yield, changeover,
downtime, team
development, business
processes, etc.)
→

Team Knowledge Processes

| Acquire or Create | Capture/ Codify | Disseminate | Apply | Renew |

In each box, list:
• What you've done
• What you haven't done
• Score (1–10;
  10 = have done very well)

team. As constructed, it is particularly helpful for taking a holistic look at the team's skill requirements and prompting people to look down the road at the team's training needs. Once completed, the skills matrix is also a very useful template for training and selection initiatives.

Figure 5-5 is an example of such a matrix. Note that in identifying all of the skills needed by your team, the focus is on both core skills and enabling skills. The enabling skills include the skill sets that each team member will need to become a leader.

FIGURE 5-5. Skills matrix.

List the required core and enabling skills as well as the team members. Then identify what level of competence each team member needs for each skill. Several possible keys are given below.

Team Members	Core Skills			Enabling Skills		

Traditional	Coaching and Experience	Detailed
A = Apprentice	C = Coach	1 = Cursory
J = Journeyman	SME = Subject Matter	2 = Novice
M = Master	Expert	3 = Familiar

What we have just described is a very different approach to knowledge management than is typically used in a team environment. We are advocating a much more comprehensive methodology that assesses the four types of knowledge all teams need; designs a training plan that is suitable to each of these types of knowledge; ensures that the team conditions are ripe for learning; builds in processes to foster the development and diffusion of critical knowledge; assesses their success; and uses a skills matrix to support a variety of team processes.

The important thing to remember, however, is that the methodology we are offering does not occur in a vacuum. Rather, it is linked to the other tools in the cultural analysis, such as the interaction network analysis, the individual needs assessment, and the voice of the team. Moreover, it is also tightly linked to the other design choices that flow from the application of the environmental scan and technical analysis, thus ensuring a holistic approach to every aspect of the team and providing it with the best possible opportunity to succeed beyond expectations.

CHALLENGES, TENSIONS, AND KEY FACTORS DURING IMPLEMENTATION

The challenge is to commit to this process. Team members have probably seen approaches in the past that sounded good but didn't accomplish anything. Usually that happens because, once the rubber meets the road, training and employee development often go by the wayside.

The team needs to recognize that knowledge management is not a program; rather, it is an essential, never-ending approach to optimizing team performance. Because the approach we are recommending is so comprehensive and holistic, but still directly links back to team performance, it is likely that people will buy into it once they understand the approach—as long as they see long-term commitment to staying the course.

The best way to "stay the course" is to institutionalize knowledge management, as we have discussed throughout this chapter. That is, incorporate knowledge management into the team's processes, procedures, and systems so that it is constantly discussed and addressed. We also recommend making your knowledge management plans visible, in the manner that we will be describing in the next chapter.

Once the topic becomes a regular part of your team's meetings and deliberations, as opposed to a once-a-year, obligatory discussion, its importance will increase and become part of the way the team does business. And the more the team's knowledge increases, the better it will perform.

HOW DEVELOPING AND MANAGING KNOWLEDGE WILL HELP BUILD LEADERS

You can't build a team of leaders if you do not provide people with the requisite skills to become leaders—it is as simple as that. Leaders are made, not born, and the best way to create a team of leaders is to create an environment and framework within which they will grow into the role. The preceding chapters of this book showed you just how to develop such an environment and framework.

By the same token, your team needs to control the way knowledge is developed and managed. Most teams make the greatest strides in the diffusion (sharing and applying knowledge) area. As teams align themselves to the organization's purpose and strategy, are organized around a conversion process (state change), have designed and aligned structures and systems, and move along the Five-Stage Team Development Model, knowledge sharing becomes an enormous pull rather than a push. It is like a strong magnet pulling knowledge throughout the team. As teams excel in increasing the knowledge capability they share across teams more freely, the whole organization benefits.

Visual Management

*Key principle: Visual management, also known
as visual performance management, is a program
that uses the senses to reinforce the previously
described principles, drive performance,
and build future leaders.*

ASSUMING YOU TAKE ALL the steps we just described in the previous chapters, you will be well on your way to having strong, self-managing teams. However, there is another innovative design element you can add to the equation to continually keep the objective of getting to and staying at Stage Five in everyone's face. Moreover, this particular innovation will support and reinforce all your design elements and help take you to another level. We call that element visual management.[1]

Simply put, visual management is a time-tested approach that combines generally accepted management principles *along with the fine arts* to improve your team's performance by 1) transforming your space into an inspiring, data-driven environment and 2) helping to elevate employees so that they become leaders. It is not a program per se; it is a conscious choice to use your space to send clear and consistent messages, support all the other team design elements, and help brand your team with its own unique environment.

YOUR CURRENT ENVIRONMENT

Take some time and go look at your current workspace through a fresh pair of eyes. What do you see? Does it help pull the team together? Does it contribute to performance improvement? Does it share important information at both the group and individual levels? Does it honor your mission and your customers? Does it celebrate the good work of you and your teammates? Does it help hold everyone accountable? Does it shape the outside world's view of your unit/team so that every time someone visits you the first reaction is, "Wow, these people are doing great things!" or "I want to work here!" We're guessing that the answer to most, if not all, of these questions is a less than enthusiastic "No," or "I don't think so."

We suspect your current space is okay. You probably have decent furniture surrounded by partitions that may be high or low. Your colors are most likely neutral and your walls may contain pictures of nature and/or reproductions of artwork.

You probably have little if any displays regarding your mission, your history, and your customers. Moreover, we doubt you have much data posted regarding your goals or performance, either at the group or individual levels. Finally, we're guessing you don't have many (if any) displays that celebrate the great work of your employees.

Does this sound like your team's workspace? If it does, consider whether this type of design contributes to producing a team of leaders. Obviously, we think it does not.

Now, imagine. Take a moment and imagine working in a space that is consciously designed to create leaders: It's a space that keeps important group performance information in view every single day and fosters discussions about how to make the team better. It's a space that shows you how you are doing and triggers conversations about how you can improve and/or help others do the same.

Think about working in an environment filled with both the history of your team as well as numerous success stories documenting how your team improved people's lives. What if that same environment celebrated the great work of you and your teammates through employee walls of fame and recognition rooms? Wouldn't such an environment elevate everyone by helping you all to see the big picture, while also showing you that everyone is truly valued?

Imagine working in an environment that is so inspiring and energizing that it makes you want to periodically bring your family and friends in to see the latest changes. Or consider having a workplace that attracts visitors like flies and makes people clamor to want to work for and with you. Finally, envision a space that is so appealing and invigorating that when outsiders come in, they immediately become excited and believe they are seeing something new and different—and instantly develop a highly favorable first impression of your team.

When this happens, everyone takes note and develops a strong feeling of pride and a greater sense of community. Instead of becoming passive followers (i.e., people who blow with the wind and stay under the radar), you and your teammates become more invested and more committed. This is what a Stage Five team *looks and feels like*.

You probably haven't seen many if any workspaces that match this description, but they exist. They don't exist by chance—they exist because a conscious decision was made to use this concept.

TELL ME MORE ABOUT VISUAL MANAGEMENT

Visual management combines sound management principles (e.g., organizational systems design, human resources management, performance management) along with the fine arts (painting, photography, sculpture, music, film) to create and sustain competitive advantage. It creates a work environment that supports and reinforces all the systems and processes we explained earlier in the book. Such an environment helps you change your culture and improve your team members' attitudes, perspectives, knowledge base, mindset, and, most important, performance.

When your space is designed to produce a team of leaders, everyone begins to see the world differently. The mission and vision become more ingrained in you and your teammates than ever before. The goals, metrics, and actual performance are there as a constant reminder of what you are trying to accomplish and how you are doing. Moreover, with the displays emphasizing the importance and accomplishments of each team member, everyone feels more valued and appreciated. As a result, people become more dedicated to the team and its mission and performance. In other words, it helps get you to Stage Five and stay there.

What used to be presumably "nice space" designed to house the team, now becomes a vibrant area replete with a series of aligned messages and information that fully supports the goal of exceptional performance delivered by a team of leaders.

Think of it as a combination of a NASA or Pentagon war room combined with the beauty and clarity of the Metropolitan Museum of Art, with a touch of Las Vegas glitz thrown in. The idea is to have the one element of the work experience *that people see all the time*—i.e., your physical space—be perfectly aligned with the other design elements so that everyone working in that space receives incredibly clear and consistent messages and information.

When you first walk into space designed with visual management principles, the images there hit you right between the eyes and convey the sense that you are doing something special. For instance, one customer contact team set up an area right outside the entrance to its offices showing video holographs of customers talking about their experiences.

Another team used to have all its file cabinets sitting next to the windows soaking in the sun, while the employees sat in the middle of the floor dodging traffic. Once the team embraced visual management, it placed the employees next to the windows and moved the cabinets to sit in front of the team as a natural barrier. Above the floor space, they placed television monitors that contained daily group performance updates. This design sent a message that every team member was important and deserved prime space and access to key information, while giving the team its own natural boundary.

That same team had a war room where everyone met to discuss how the team was performing and to review variances in individual performance and attendance. Imagine how focused those meetings must have been!

In yet a different team, the leader sits right in the middle of the workspace with no partitions or barriers, even though other team members have offices. The clear message here is that the leader's role is one of support, not dominance—a sign of a Stage Five team.

The types of images and displays we have just mentioned will improve communication and teamwork, knowledge and understanding, engagement and commitment, responsibility and accountability, and innovation and creativity, all of which will elevate the employees and the team and drive performance. That is exactly what visual management is all about.

VISUAL MANAGEMENT AND THE BRAIN

Before we delve further into the concept, we'd like you to step back and think of you and your teammates' mental processing preferences and the possibilities that visual management offers you.

According to the theory of brain dominance, each side of the brain controls different ways of thinking. Under this theory, people on your team prefer one way of thinking over the other. For instance, a left-brained person's preferences tend to be more logical, analytical, and objective, while a right-brained person tends to be more intuitive, emotional, and subjective.[2]

With respect to learning, Herrmann International, the originator of Whole Brain Thinking, writes that "each one of us as a learner is a unique human being with a unique learning style. Consider your own experience:

You likely did much better in some subjects than others; surely you responded much more to some teaching methods than others; finally, you retained some material more accurately and for a longer period of time than other material delivered in a different way."[3]

Visual management uses a Whole Brain approach that speaks to all your team's members, regardless of their different work and learning preferences. This is accomplished by communicating through the use of strategically placed charts, graphs, tables, words, pictures, paintings, statues, artifacts, video, and music. Such an approach provides you with an enormous opportunity to connect each and every team member to both the team and its mission and ensure that your messages appeal to everyone—regardless of their brain dominance or learning preference.

By the same token, this Whole Brain approach also helps capture the hearts and minds of your team, which will help propel you to Stage Five. It works because, in our experience, the three best ways to facilitate long-term memory are through significant emotional experiences, music, and the use of metaphors.[4] If you want to optimize visual management, you can and should incorporate all three of these elements into your displays.

SO WHAT WILL VISUAL MANAGEMENT DO FOR US?

Based on our experience and the feedback of others who have used this approach, if you properly implement visual management, it will:

- Help you and your teammates feel, see, hear, and touch the mission, vision, core values, and results required to gain competitive advantage and improve performance.

- Prompt the team to focus on critical information in ways that cannot be ignored.

- Encourage everyone to deal with your problems and challenges, including individual employee performance problems.

- Reinforce your success.

- Help you take pride in what you do.

- Make the work more meaningful and fun.

- Positively shape the way that the outside world views your team, its contribution, and prospects.

- Influence the way you and your teammates think, feel, learn, and act, and ultimately make you a team of leaders.

Later on in this chapter, we'll show you how and why teams can reap these benefits, when we share several examples of teams that have used visual management to get to Stage Five and drive improved performance!

IS VISUAL MANAGEMENT WORTH IT?

We suspect that by now you recognize that visual management can make a difference. We also believe you can now see how it helps grow leaders in your team. Finally, we trust you have come to the conclusion that building a team of leaders actually does help to improve performance and address the challenges we referenced in the first chapter.

However, some of you may also be thinking, "With everything else you are suggesting we do in the other chapters, do we really need to also add visual management to our team development model?" The answer is simply this: You do not have to do it, but if you do it properly, it will provide you with all the aforementioned benefits. All these benefits have been documented by teams/organizations that have used visual management, and we will share these results with you later on in this chapter.

First, let's discuss how visual management started and the benefits it produces.

HOW VISUAL MANAGEMENT BEGAN

In September 1994, Stew became the director of the U.S. Department of Veterans Affairs' Los Angeles Regional Office (LARO), which employed more than 400 employees, had a budget of about $18 million, and served roughly 1.2 million veterans. At the time, this office had an extremely poor reputation for performance. Out of fifty-seven offices, the LARO had the lowest customer satisfaction score for processing compensation and pension claims; only forty-six veterans who applied for vocational rehabilitation were considered to have been rehabilitated; and the office had thousands of foreclosed properties in its inventory. There was also low morale, high turnover, and a rate of granting compensation and pension benefits that was 50 percent below the nation, which was the lowest within the Department of Veterans Affairs (that means a veteran applying for benefits in Los Angeles was 50 percent less likely to have a claim granted than at the average regional office around the country).

When he arrived, Stew was particularly struck by several things: 1) The employees tended to be very cynical, and many looked for reasons to *deny* rather than grant benefits; 2) the office had little if any accountability, contributing to a belief among the employees that management was not serious about high performance; and 3) although the LARO was located in a federal building that was more than adequate, the space itself was shoddy, unkempt, and unprofessional. As you might imagine, the employees performed and behaved accordingly.

As part of his overall strategy for turning that office around, Stew wanted to create a team environment. Along these lines, he sought out advice on organizational design from Paul, who emphasized the importance of taking a holistic approach to the transformation effort (i.e., teams could not be created in a vacuum).

Shortly thereafter, Stew had an idea. He felt that if they could redesign the physical plant in order to honor the contributions of veterans, they might begin to change the culture of the LARO office. Being a classically trained fine artist with an eye for how things fit together, he knew how to redesign space. He therefore began this effort by having his staff hang up some photographs depicting the veteran's experience. It immediately proved to be a big hit.

However, the real breakthrough came when it dawned on him that the key was not to focus exclusively on veterans and make the space look better; it was to *transform the space* using a balanced approach so that the culture and the employees' mindset would change, leading to better results. He had to marry the fine arts with 1) the organizational design principles that Paul had taught him and 2) human resources management and performance management principles.

This meant not only hanging up photographs and works of art about the customer (veterans), but also displaying focused information about performance—at the station, team, and individual levels—while also celebrating many of the daily accomplishments that were heretofore unknown. It meant establishing a physical plant that reinforced the exact same messages that Stew and his team were trying to send to the troops through their management systems.

Figure 6-1 shows the roadmap that the LARO used to reinforce those messages.

As the LARO moved forward, it developed a virtual museum of veterans' benefits throughout the workspace, set up private reflection areas depicting the veterans' experience, and displayed large, inspiring artifacts, such as a helicopter, a U-2 cockpit, a jeep, a cannon, and scale models of a submarine and tank. The regional office also installed a series of displays that conveyed both real-time and daily performance and rewards information, and posted most team members' individual performance. Figure 6-2 is a photograph of one of its entrance areas.

It is important to recognize that visual management was not implemented as a stand-alone program. After all, while this work was ongoing, units were being transformed into teams and supervisors became coaches, with about half of the former supervisors being replaced. A heavy emphasis was placed on communication and accountability, and many of the management systems and processes were aligned to these objectives.

The impact of visual management, in conjunction with the many other changes/design elements that were implemented, was that the employees/teams changed their mindset and became elevated and much more focused on the mission and the team's success. The overall grant

FIGURE 6-1. LARO roadmap.

FIGURE 6-2. Redesigned entrance (welcome) area.

rate increased by 50 percent, the customer satisfaction rate increased by 37 percent, the number of veterans rehabilitated went up by 600 percent, and the number of foreclosed properties in inventory plummeted.

The LARO's success was nationally recognized in 2001, when it received the prestigious PILLAR (Performance Incentives Leadership Linked to Achieving Results) Award from the United States Office of Personnel Management.

VISUAL MANAGEMENT SPREADS

As word of this concept grew, other VA regional offices began to adopt at least some of its components. For example, the Honolulu Regional Office developed its own roadmap (see Figure 6-3) and used many of the same design elements.

Other VA medical centers also began to take notice, with the VA Central California Health Care System being the greatest proponent of

FIGURE 6-3. Honolulu Regional Office roadmap.

the concept. For example, it sent a few teams to the LARO and thereafter developed its own program, believing it could have a similar impact within healthcare. This medical center used the concept "to inspire VA patients, visitors, and staff through visual images." In the words of the director at the time, Al Perry, FACHE:

The images set the stage and establish a tone for superb customer service, pride in work, and honor of military service. The program has steadily grown, becoming bolder and more creative and colorful each year. Staff, patients, and visitors speak highly of the very positive effect it has on them!

Over the last eleven years, we have carefully added 'images' of patriotism, military service, superb care, and wellness in the form of photographs, paintings, murals, displays, and flags….

Patients have commented that the visual management program has given them a sense of sanctuary, caring, and deep respect. Staff have commented on the pride it gives them to serve veterans.[5]

Has visual management had an impact? Certainly, in terms of setting a tone for other interior and exterior aesthetics and level of cleanliness, it most definitely has. (See Figure 6-4 for an interior view.) There is a theme of pride, honor, and service that is reinforced in all interior and exterior areas of the medical center, as well in local VA advertising and other media campaigns. Because of the visually managed tone, patients expect respectful, superb care, and the staff strives daily to provide it. Visual reminders are everywhere.

… [W]e also believe visual management has contributed in some degree to ever-higher performance over the years. Some examples: In 2003, two years after beginning the program, VA received Fresno's prestigious Excellence in Business Award for healthcare. Employee satisfaction surveys show, in sixteen measured areas, scores 100 percent above national VA averages in 2006–2009. In 2007, VA won the

FIGURE 6-4. Inside the VA's Central California Health Care System.

agency's Diversity Award and Labor Management Award. In 2008, we were voted by staff the "Fifth Best Company to Work for in Central California." In 2009, the medical center achieved a ranking of fourth highest among 139 VA [medical centers] nationwide, based on measured quality, access, and satisfaction; and, in 2010, we won a Carey Award [the VA's equivalent to the Baldrige Award].[6]

The concept also spread outside VA. When Bronco Mendenhall first took over as head coach of the Brigham Young University (BYU) football program, the walls were blank and covered with white paint. Inspired by the book *Seeing Is Believing*,[7] Bronco set out to use the walls of the Student Athlete Building as a medium on which to deliver information about the team's mission, history, aspirations and culture.… When visual messages are aligned with the talk of organization leaders, the [visual] underscores the aural, and vice versa. Because skillful visual management keeps people focused in what is important, it improves performance across the board.[8]

Among other things, Bronco built a Home of Champions Wall, a tribute to its bowl history; an NFL wall; a Called to Serve display (see Figure 6-5), which depicts where members of the football team have served or are serving as missionaries throughout the world; and a meeting room detailing the BYU football players' achievements and aspirations, with cardboard shields drawn by players, expressing their priorities, affections, and hopes.[9]

Prior to Bronco taking the reins of BYU's football team, the team had experienced three straight losing seasons. After initially leading them to a 6–6 record, Bronco continued to lead his players into record-setting

FIGURE 6-5. BYU's "Called to Serve" display.

territory. The team won between ten and eleven games per season during the next five out of six years, something that BYU had never before achieved in its history.[10] While visual management is obviously not the only reason for BYU's success, it was clearly used as part of an overall performance improvement strategy that has proved to be wildly successful.

Wouldn't your team like to enjoy the same successes as the teams we've described? Here's how to do it.

HOW TO IMPLEMENT VISUAL MANAGEMENT

Start by establishing a visual management team made up of representatives of your team and perhaps some experts outside the team (e.g., someone from building management or facilities management, information technology, even an internal or external consultant). In this way, it won't be one person's plan; it will be the team's plan. Moreover, you'll gain differing perspectives, which should make the process of implementing the plan richer and more inclusive.

Keep in mind that once a decision is made to move forward, your team will need one overarching vision for its space; otherwise, it is likely to be a mishmash. The team leader, or someone above him or her in the organization, should initially be a champion of the concept, since that person should be someone who wields a high degree of organizational clout. In this way, you stand a greater chance of getting the concept off the ground without meeting too much organizational resistance.

The visual management team is a great place to model how a team can move along the five-stage continuum. It will provide members with a series of wonderful opportunities to engage in a variety of important tasks. Just as important, you can expect most, if not all, of your team members to step up and assume leadership in one or more key areas of visual management.

You should implement visual management in two stages: 1) planning/ building a foundation and 2) the actual implementation. Within the first stage, there are two established phases; within the second, there are four. This is not intended to be a rigid and inflexible process, since you probably have at least some of the key elements already in place. You should instead view the process as a logical way to approach your planning and implementation—but with the understanding that 1) you should focus your team's time and energy on the phases where it is most needed, and 2) your goal is always to take your team to Stage Five.

PLANNING AND BUILDING A FOUNDATION

Phase One: Planning. Before you implement visual management, make sure your mission, vision, values, and systems are aligned using the team systems design model we introduced in Chapter 2. After all, you don't want to reinforce a set of contradictory messages. Once you do that, make sure that visual management is right for your team. That is, will the team members support the concept? Will they be in it for the long haul? Will it be a good fit for the culture you are trying to build? Don't waste your time on the concept if the answers to these questions are negative.

Assuming you decide to go forward, this would be a good time for you to develop some form of a visual roadmap and/or mission/vision/ values statement that will show how you will get to Stage Five. A roadmap will get the ball rolling and let the team know you are serious about going down this path.

Phase Two: Building a framework. Next, you begin to educate the team on the importance of visual management and introduce its benefits. You might begin by providing the team with reading material about the concept, bringing in experts in the field to make presentations, and/or visiting a team/organization that is already using the concept. Bear in mind that you don't want to move too quickly for fear of the team rejecting the concept due to a lack of understanding.

If any of your systems and/or processes are out of line, now is the time to make adjustments (you should be modifying your systems/processes concurrently with all the other design work necessary to ultimately get you to Stage Five). While the natural tendency is to immediately begin to put up displays, we strongly recommend you hold off until the proper foundation is in place.

You need to audit and assess the physical plant to determine whether the supporting elements are in place. Is the lighting appropriate? Are the colors effective? Are there any design accents? How's the carpet? Is there too much clutter? What about the ergonomics? Most important, is the space set up in a way that will help get your team to Stage Five?

IMPLEMENTATION

Phase Three: Creating the space. To begin, you review the workflow. For example, are the essential adjacencies in place? (That is, are the right people situated next to each other?) Is there a good fit between the physical plant and the management systems? Are your furniture, cabinets, and shelves functional? Are your partitions the right height? (Make note: High partitions often inhibit teamwork.)

You should also review the decision-making and information systems. Do your team members know what is going on? What are the best places to display metrics? Once you assess these issues, you develop a plan for displaying group and individual performance.

You want to ask yourself if the space is helping to drive the right behaviors. That is, are people enthusiastically greeting visitors? Do they have a sense of urgency? Do they have a high amount of energy? Are they working hard? Of course, these issues should also be addressed whenever you are looking at your systems and processes and your culture.

Finally, you are ready to begin repainting and changing the lights and/or the carpets if necessary, to ensure you have the proper foundation for future displays. Very simply, there is no point hanging displays in dark areas or in an environment where the carpet sucks the life out of your space.

Phase Four: Focusing on customers and data. Here is where the fun begins. With the foundation set and all the analyses completed, now you get serious about hanging your team's displays. Typically, you start with two key areas: 1) your mission, customers, and suppliers, and 2) the metrics.

With respect to the former, your team should start by highlighting its mission (what it is all about) and who it is here to serve (the customers). These displays may include history exhibits and/or success stories. They may also contain information about some of your key products and/or services. Expect these displays to get everyone's attention, with more team members seeking to get involved in the process.

During phase four, your data displays may expand in the form of war rooms, computer monitors, and bulletin boards. War rooms are generally used at higher levels in the organization. However, if the team has the space and the wherewithal to establish one, by all means they should do so. Expect these displays to trigger more interest in group performance and foster a lot of positive internal discussions, although some low performers may not be as enchanted with the concept. This is the phase when you will really begin to see a difference in the team that will help drive you to Stage Five.

Phase Five: Focusing on employees and fine-tuning the details. In this phase, you begin to home in on the employees and your people system, while continuing to build out other displays. For example, you can start to post individual employee performance data (as discussed in Chapter 4).

You'll also want to ensure that rewards and recognition information is linked and posted. After all, the more tightly rewards are linked to other key elements, the more effective they will be. Furthermore, this is the occasion to visually celebrate the great work of the team in the form of walls of fame, team members of the month, and candid photos of the employees in action.

Finally, this would be a good time for you to try and take your displays to another level. For instance, you should consider going beyond pictures, boards, and monitors and add some three-dimensional objects such as artifacts, kiosks, and maybe even statues. You may also want to go beyond visual displays and start appealing to the other senses. If appropriate, consider incorporating sound (e.g., music, voice recordings), tactile displays (e.g., that team members can feel, sit in, or stand on), and smells. Appealing to all the senses—sight, hearing, touch, smell, and even taste—will deepen your team's emotional connection to the mission and each other.

By now, don't be surprised if word of your team's visual displays reaches the outside world and triggers a rash of visitors. Such visits will provide you with an additional sense of pride that your team is truly doing something special.

Phase Six: Renewal. Here is where your team renews its displays. Renewal entails assessing whether visual management is accomplishing what it was intended to do. Is it working well? Is it having a positive impact on performance? How do people feel about it? Does it need to be refreshed?

This is a good time to determine whether the displays are still aligned with the team's mission, direction, and technology or if adjustments need to be made. It is also a good idea to periodically rotate the displays in order to ensure that people are still seeing them and paying attention to them.

At this phase, you should consider changing some of the visual management team members as well. After all, on occasion it is good to get fresh ideas and new perspectives.

Finally, you might want to visit other sites that have similar approaches, so you can steal shamelessly from them. Another approach would be to invite one or more experts on the topic to visit your facilities, review your displays, and suggest new and exciting options to experiment with, moving forward. Whatever approach you take will ensure that visual management stays vibrant, continues to grow, and, most important, helps your team reach and stay at Stage Five.

HOW VISUAL MANAGEMENT IMPACTS ON AND EVOLVES WITH EVERY STAGE OF TEAM DEVELOPMENT

Visual management's six phases of planning and implementation provide terrific opportunities for your team to grow as it moves along the five stages of team development. As everyone grasps the principles behind visual management, it will become easier for team members to step up and take responsibility for the key activities and tasks along the way.

The first four phases of visual management planning/implementation generally occur at about the same pace that your team goes through the first four development stages. After all, the initial phases/stages involve a heavy degree of planning, analysis, and training and, to some extent, cover the same ground, while the last phases/stages are where the rubber meets the road. Eventually, when your team evolves to Stage Five, your visual management program will probably be in the fine-tuning phase and, possibly, the final renewal phase.

However, recognize that it is also okay for your team to be in a different phase of visual management than its corresponding stage of team development. It may be that the foundation (e.g., lights, color, furniture) is already in place and assessed to be fine, or much of the data may already have been posted, and priorities often dictate how much can be accomplished at any one time. Keep in mind that if all the planning is done right, everything will eventually fall into place and align.

The key here is that you recognize that everything is connected and that the entire plan needs to move forward in a holistic manner.

CHALLENGES, TENSIONS, AND KEY
FACTORS DURING IMPLEMENTATION

Anytime you try and implement something new, there are always challenges and often pushbacks. Implementing visual management is no exception.

The first question that may be raised is, "Why are you planning to spend a lot of time and energy on an interior decoration program? Don't we have better things to do?" Expect to hear this question in the early phases because at least some members of the team probably won't immediately grasp the concept or understand how it fits in the overall scheme. The best way to respond to this concern is through education. Explain the concept to them. Emphasize that it is a performance improvement program, *not* an interior design or artsy-fartsy approach. Provide people with some of the written material on visual management, and point them toward some success stories. They will eventually get it.

A good tactic is to include at least some of the skeptics on the visual management team. As they learn more about the concept and get sucked into the whole process, it is very likely that they will convert to being champions of the program.

Another question that is bound to come up is, "How do you plan on paying for it?" The Los Angeles Regional Office of the Veterans Administration spent about $300,000 on the program. However, the vast majority of the work was not paid for by government funds. Instead, the money came in the form of donations from veterans' groups that immediately saw the potential impact of visual management on their clients. Moreover, the employees gave many of the artifacts, displays, and exhibits to the office as a gift. How often does that happen?

On the other hand, many other teams have implemented visual management on a shoestring budget. After all, it doesn't have to cost much money to post data or hang pictures of your customers and employees. There are many creative ways in which to finance visual management, too. (For example, at the LARO, Stew traded providing HRM advice to one organization for one of its Civil War cannons.) The options are endless and are only limited by your imagination and final budget.

A good way of thinking about visual management is to recall the famous line from *Field of Dreams*: "If you build it, they will come." In other words, if you do visual management well, once the displays start to go up, people—including your team members—will come forward to contribute their time, personal skills, artifacts, and memorabilia, and sometimes even money, to the cause.

HOW VISUAL MANAGEMENT WILL HELP BUILD LEADERS

By surrounding yourself with an environment that honors your mission and customers, you will be more connected to those you serve. By visually celebrating the good work of your team and its members, you and your peers will feel appreciated and believe you are part of something special. By providing everyone with all the information they need to know in order to succeed, you will all understand what is happening and what you have to do.

By having a visual and transparent system of accountability, everyone will see that there are reliable consequences for every level of performance and behavior and that the team is truly committed to winning. Finally, by having an environment that attracts and enamors the outside world in such a way that people view the team as being cutting-edge and wildly successful, you and your team will feel a genuine sense of pride and ownership.

When all these things happen, people become elevated. They are no longer merely disposable workers; instead, they are energized, knowledgeable, and inspired, and they take a keen interest in ensuring that the team succeeds. In short, they are a Stage Five team of leaders.

CONCLUSION

While Paul was growing up, his father worked as an engineer. Even as a young boy, he noticed that when things were good for his father at work, he came home in a good mood. On good days, he wanted to play catch or golf at Smiley's golfing range. When things were bad, he would give Paul and other family members a hard time, asking, "Why didn't you do this or that?"

When Paul's dad liked working with the people at his company and they pulled their own weight, he came home happy. When work was meaningful, his father was motivated. When he was learning something new, he was energized.

When work wasn't enjoyable—when his father was doing the same old thing or supervisors were more interested in whether the i's were dotted and the t's were crossed—he was miserable. Paul came to realize that the work his father performed had a major impact on him and the family. He began to wonder why things couldn't be better for his dad at work so that he could be happier and have a positive impact on Paul and the entire Gustavson family at home.

More than fifty years later, things haven't changed all that much. For example, according to Gallup's 2013 State of the American Workplace Report, "Just 30 percent of employees are engaged and inspired at work … the rest … not so much. A little more than half of workers (52 percent) have a perpetual case of the Mondays—they're present, but not particularly excited about their job." Gallup further found that disengaged employees cost the United States as much as *$550 billion* per year in lost productivity.[1]

That is exactly why this book is so timely and important. The same ways of doing business simply won't work in the twenty-first century. People want to be involved, challenged, and empowered. They want to be part of something that is bigger than them, and they want to make a difference. Moreover, they want to continue to grow and develop.

They don't want to work for a boss who tells them to keep their mouths shut and do as they are told. They don't want to do work that is boring and inconsequential, and they certainly don't want to be merely spokes in a wheel that can be replaced at the drop of a hat. Unfortunately, the reality is that far too many people feel that way in the workplace.

The consequences of a work culture/environment where people are disengaged and can't wait for the weekend are devastating, not only in terms of lost or reduced productivity, but also in higher turnover, lower organizational energy, and reduced employee commitment.

Fortunately, there is a better way of doing business. As we have shown you throughout this book, turning everyone into a leader using the Five-Stage Team Development Model is a win-win situation for all concerned. Your employees will be more engaged, more involved, and more excited.

They will work within a team design that is logical, efficient, and well aligned, and they will use processes that have relatively few downstream variances. In addition, they will develop far more skills than they currently have and understand the value they contribute to their team and the organization. Finally, they will work within an environment they are proud of, as well as one that helps people perform better, holds everyone accountable, and positively influences the outside world.

From a manager's point of view, you will get better performance, greater productivity, increased profits, and higher customer and employee satisfaction. Furthermore, instead of trying to manage the employees, they will manage themselves—and with more energy and enthusiasm than you could ever hope to have under a traditional work arrangement. These positive effects will, of course, free you up to do the work you always wanted to do but never seemed to have the time.

Moreover, as word gets out about the cutting-edge changes you are making and your accompanying success, expect to be inundated with requests from the outside world to learn more about your new approach. That is not a bad position to be in, is it?

Creating a team/organization of leaders is not an easy thing to do—if so, everyone would have done it by now. However, it is the *right thing to do* for all of the reasons we've described throughout the book. A team of leaders will both produce the results you are looking for and make the work experience much more exciting and enjoyable for everybody … and now is the time to get started.

If you apply the various strategies, tools, and techniques you need to create high-performance teams, in the manner we've described, you will take your team/organization to a whole new level. We wish you the best of luck on your journey.

Notes

INTRODUCTION

1. Charles Fishman, "Engines of Democracy," *Fast Company,* no. 28, October 1999, www.fastcompany.com/37815/engines-democracy.

2. "GE Aviation Durham Expands and Invests for the Future," news release, October 12, 2010, www.geaviation.com/press/other/other_20101012.html, retrieved January 29, 2013.

3. Fishman, "Engines of Democracy."

4. For more information on the VA's New York Regional Office receiving the first Hammer Award, see "National Partnership for Reinventing Government," http://govinfo.library.unt.edu/npr/library/announc/hamrpart2.html, retrieved January 29, 2013, and "Vice President Gore Hits Home with HAMMER Award for VA Regional Office," U.S. Office of Personnel Management, http://archive.opm.gov/perform/articles/097.asp, retrieved January 29, 2013.

CHAPTER 1: CREATING ADVANTAGE THROUGH THE FIVE-STAGE TEAM DEVELOPMENT MODEL

1. "A History of Innovation," Herrmann International, www.hbdi.com/WhyUs/history.php, retrieved August 31, 2012.

2. "The Herrmann Brain Dominance Instrument (HBDI)," www.hbdi.com/uploads/100046_Brochures/100678.pdf, retrieved August 31, 2012.

3. See Kerry Patterson et al., *Crucial Conversations: Tools for Talking When Stakes Are High* (New York: McGraw-Hill, 2002).

4. Stephen M. R. Covey and Rebecca R. Merrill, *The Speed of Trust: The One Thing That Changes Everything* (New York: Free Press, 2008).

5. See Dyer & Associates, dyerteambuilding.com/about-us.php, retrieved September 4, 2012. William G. Dyer was former dean of the Marriott School of Management and founder of the Department of Organizational Behavior at Brigham Young University (BYU). He served as a private consultant to many companies and was the author of numerous books and articles on organizational change and team dynamics.

6. Etienne Wegner, "Communities of Practice: A Brief Introduction," www.ewenger.com/theory, retrieved September 4, 2012.

7. For this section, we relied in part on *Cultivating Communities of Practice*, by Etienne Wenger, Richard McDermott, and William M. Snyder (Boston: Harvard Business School Publishing, 2002).

8. The section on customer value added (CVA) was influenced by the work of Mark Rhodes (see www.strategybydesign.org) and the book *Managing Customer Value: Creating Quality and Service That Customers Can See*, by Bradley T. Gale (New York: Free Press, 1994).

CHAPTER 2: SECRETS OF GREAT DESIGN

1. This description was based on an unpublished case study written by Mark Rhodes.

CHAPTER 4: TEAM VALUE CREATION MODEL

1. Jack Stack, *The Great Game of Business, Unlocking the Power and Profitability of Open-Book Management* (New York: Doubleday, 1994).

2. Jack Stack, "That Championship Season," *Inc. Magazine*, July 1996.

3. Patricia Amend, "The Turnaround: How a Dying Division of International Harvester Became One of America's Most Competitive Small Companies," *Inc. Magazine*, August 1986.

4. Ned Hermann, "The Theory Behind the HBDI and Whole Brain Technology," Herrmann International, www.hbdi.com/uploads/100024_articles/100543. pdf, retrieved August 22, 2012.

1. Knowledge development capabilities in our team development model have been influenced by the work of William M. Snyder, Ph.D. His biography can be found at www.organizationdesign.com.

1. For more detailed information on the concept of visual management, see Stewart Liff and Pamela A. Posey, *Seeing Is Believing: How the New Art of Visual Management Can Boost Performance Throughout Your Organization* (New York: AMACOM Books, 2004); Stewart Liff, "Using Visual Management to Improve Performance," and "Designing Your Space Using Visual Management," *OhMyGov* (blog), http://blog.ohmygov. com/members/StewLiff.aspx, retrieved December 4, 2012; Stewart Liff, "Shaping Space for Success: The Power of Visual Management," *The Public Manager,* Spring 2012, www.thepublicmanager.org/docs_articles/ current/Vol41,2012/Vol41,Issue01/Vol41N1_shapingspacefor.pdf; Matt Bristol, "Lessons in Liberty," *VA Vanguard Magazine,* July/August 2002, www.va.gov/opa/publications/archives/vanguard/02julaugvg.pdf; and Brian Friel, "Seeing Is Believing," *Government Executive Magazine,* July 1, 2002, www.govexec.com/magazine/2002/07/seeing-is-believing/11941/.

2. Kendra Cherry, "Left Brain vs. Right Brain," *About.com Psychology,* http:// psychology.about.com/od/cognitivepsychology/a/left-brain-right-brain.htm, retrieved December 27, 2012. Roger W. Sperry, who won the Nobel Prize for his work in this area in 1981, originally pioneered the concept.

3.   Ann Herrmann-Nehdi, "The Best of Both Worlds—Making Blended Learning Really Work by Engaging the Whole Brain," Herrmann International white paper, www.hbdi.com/uploads/100016_whitepapers/100607.pdf, retrieved December 27, 2012.

4.   "An Interview and Giveaway with Paul Gustavson, Author of Running into the Wind," *Fire and Ice* (blog), August 30, 2012, http://fireandicephoto. blogspot.com/2012/08/interview-giveaway-with-paul-gustavson.html, retrieved December 27, 2012. The idea discussed in this article originated with Ned Herrmann.

5.   The quote from Al Perry was first cited in Stewart Liff's article, "Shaping Space for Success: The Power of Visual," *The Public Manager*.

6.   Stewart Liff, "Shaping Space for Success: The Power of Visual."

7.   Stewart Liff and Pamela A. Posey, *Seeing Is Believing* (New York: AMACOM Books, 2004).

8.   Paul Gustavson and Alyson Von Feldt, *Running into the Wind: Bronco Mendenhall—5 Strategies for Building a Successful Team* (Salt Lake City: Shadow Mountain, 2012).

9.   Ibid.

10. Ibid.

CONCLUSION

1.   Kelli B. Grant, "Americans Hate Their Jobs, Even with Perks," *USA Today*, June 30, 2013.

Index